Best Regards,

Harold B Simpson

Nothing but flags! but simple flags,
Tattered and torn and hanging in rags;
And we walk beneath them with careless tread,
Nor think of the hosts of the mighty dead
Who have marched beneath them in days gone by.

—Moses Owen (1838-1878)

SIX FLAGS OF TEXAS

Introduction by
Governor John Connally

Foreword by
Joe B. Frantz

Original Paintings by
Donald M. Yena

James M. Day

Richard G. Santos

Ben Procter

Harold B. Simpson

Rupert N. Richardson

Dorman H. Winfrey

49496

| TEXIAN PRESS | 1968 | WACO, TEXAS |

Library of Congress Catalog Card Number
68 - 57365

First Edition

Published
by

P. O. Box 1684
Waco, Texas

———

Bound by
Library Binding Co.
Waco, Texas

This book is dedicated to the men who served their
country and their flag. In victory and defeat they did
their duty, leaving us a priceless heritage.

Introduction

"I am a part of all that I have met," wrote the poet, and the Texan today is indeed demonstrative of that truth. In this year of nineteen hundred and sixty-eight, the State has opened a magnificent new building in San Antonio which proudly shows the contributions of twenty-five different peoples who have come to Texas. They have stayed to become a part of our makeup, and hence, of our colorful history.

Another important factor in the molding of Texans is the six actual changes of sovereignty through which we have passed. *Six Flags of Texas* deals with these eras—each sharp with event, each singular in its presentation of the varied opportunities to be found here. Donald Yena's graphic paintings depict great moments of drama within the periods, while moving texts are contributed by eminent historians. They include Dr. Rupert N. Richardson, Dr. Ben Procter, Dr. Dorman Winfrey, Dr. James M. Day, Richard G. Santos, and Colonel Harold B. Simpson.

This volume is in keeping with previous books of the Texian Press that have capsuled in appealing form stories of the heroes, missions, forts and battles of Texas.

John Connally

John Connally

Governor of Texas

Foreword

Texas is not the only state that has come to the present under six flags. However, the Texas affection for its six flags is unmatched in intensity and enduring devotion. This despite the fact that the claim of one of the flags, the French, is quite tentative; while the flag of another nation, the Confederate States of America, represents a devilish aberration from political and constitutional sanity.

On the other hand, the French, as is proper for a nation which virtually invented *amour,* is highly romantic. What beautiful inefficiency blew La Salle hundreds of miles beyond the mouth of the Mississippi. What grand design made France think that this straggling little fort could be the springboard for an empire! The sheer audacity of the idea is appealing, even while we know that it never should have been taken seriously by the Spanish or anyone else.

The Spanish, of course, are another story. New Spain more or less occupied and claimed Texas for twice as long as the United States and Anglo-Americans have had it. Judged by time alone, Texas is Spanish. Considering the geographical and spacial problems, the Spanish were remarkably ineffective in their rule of Texas. True, the Indians only liked to be Christians during the periods when they couldn't live off the land, and the mission system was largely a failure. But no one came into Spanish Texas and lasted until the Mexicans came at them from within. Certainly the old families in Texas are all Spanish-American, and any Anlo-American claim to antiquity won't stand up alongside someone named Herrera or Salinas.

As for the Mexicans, they gave us a taste of liberalism and independence. Although liberalism has operated *sub rosa* from time to time in Texas, it has been a continuing thread that has brought progress to the state. Texans like to get on with things, which is our heritage from a Mexico that, chronically revolutionizing though it might be, nonetheless was dedicated to overthrowing stand-pat, oppressive leadership. There is no way of knowing whether more sage administration of Texas could have held this vast Southwest within the Mexican orbit, but undoubtedly one of the reasons Mexico lost Texas was sheer generosity admixed with neglect. The troubles of Texas *vis-a-vis* Mexico with the troubles of internal Mexico herself. When she could not govern herself, Mexico couldn't begin to retain Texas.

The Republic, of course, is the glorious period. It is to Texas what Lexington and Concord are to Massachusetts, what 1066 is to the British, what October is to modern Russia. It gave Texas an early experience that none of her neighbors to the north or west were to know for another half century, giving us a political sophistication that places us away ahead of the remainder of the West. It also gave Texas its unique flavor. Except for Hawaii, no other state in the Union was every truly independent, though some may claim their moments. But Texas stumbled and survived for ten years on her own, so that her citizens have always felt a certain independence toward the remainder of the United States. In this book we are particularly fortunate in having a Dean of Texas historians, Dr. Rupert N. Richardson, writing on what has now become the grandfather of all Texas subjects.

Some people will argue that Texas never really joined the United States, either emotionally or actually. Most of the time Texas has been a good ally or affiliate of the United States, has participated in national affairs, but has insisted on retaining a maverick personality. That last adjective, incidentally, is typical of Texas. They think the word *maverick* originated in Texas, and that the Maverick family sprang full-blown out of a Texas cactus plant or was dropped from a mesquite bean. Actually the Mavericks hit New England on the heels of the Pilgrim fathers, and East Boston is not at all self-conscious nor Texas-oriented about having one of its subway stops called Maverick Station.

One Texan, loaded with what modern pundits call charisma, reached true statesmanship during the Confederate period. Read Sam Houston's speeches and letters from the time that dark disunion first loomed on the Texas horizon in the 1850's down until the day that Texas disgracefully rejected him. Few utterances by the most impassioned American statesman can match Houston's speeches during this period for incisive clarity and intelligent devotion to the American ideal. He is one of the few Texans who really deserves the accolade GREAT.

The truth is, while most people assign the melting pot idea to the teeming cities of the east and the north, Texas is every bit as much a melting pot as Manhattan or Chicago. Texans are Indians, Mexicans, Spaniards, Frenchmen, Germans, Poles, Czechs, Swedes, British, Chinese, Negroes, Arabs, Greeks, and so on and on. We have had all the traditional successes of a melting pot, pluralistic culture; and we have had all the strains and stresses. Somehow all these races and nationalities have come together and have lived under one or more of these six flags. Some hyper-patriots have tried to make Texans out as a special breed, but the truth is that Texans are people—people from all over the world,

x

operating at every level from the wretched edge of misery to the profligate super-prosperous. Somewhere in between are most of us, reasonably happy, reasonably ambitious, and reasonably envious. We believe that the American dream is a Texas dream. We like Texas, indeed cherish it.

We think the history of Texas under six flags deserves the attention awarded it, so long as it remains accurate and in good taste. The publisher has here brought together six men who have the taste and the historical sagacity to wave six flags properly. This kind of flag-waving I can, and do, support.

Joe B. Frantz
Austin, Texas

Donald M. Yena

The featured artist in this book is no stranger to readers of Texian Press nor to serious western art collectors of Texas and the Southwest. He is Donald M. Yena, the San Antonio artist who illustrated the previous book of this series, *The Battles of Texas*. It was his stirring and unforgettable depiction of the most famous battles in Texas history that prompted his selection as the first repeating artist for the series.

Don, as he is known to his many friends, came to Texas at the age of three and grew up near the Alsation community of Castroville. Learning to sketch early in childhood, by the time he reached San Antonio's Vocational and Technical High School he had decided to become an artist. After high school he enrolled in the Hunter School of Commercial Art but his studies were interrupted in 1956 by a tour of duty with the United States Navy. While on leave the following year, he married his high school sweetheart, Miss Louise Marie Cowan. Still in the Navy but determined to become an artist, he enrolled in a correspondence course of the Famous Artists School and received a Certificate of Completion in 1962. Meanwhile, he had been released from the service in 1960 and had returned to San Antonio to launch his career as a free-lance artist. The paintings of Donald M. Yena have since begun to decorate the walls of numerous homes and business establishments throughout Texas and the United States.

The Paintings

That fateful day in March 1685 in which the *Founding of Fort Saint Louis* occurred is aptly depicted about its courageous commander Robert Cavelier, Sieur de la Salle. Acting a thousand parts from master planner to laborer, La Salle oversees the construction of the fort on the La Vaca River near historic Matagorda Bay. The busy atmosphere full of shouted orders, disgruntled curses, children's voices at play, and the hammering, chipping, sawing noises of construction are counter-balanced by La Salle's apprehension of danger and immortality in the air.

The Capture of the Nolan Expedition on March 4, 1801, is shown at the moment the North American filibusterers surrendered to the Spanish forces commanded by Captain Felipe Ecay Musquiz. With unbelieving despondency, the surviving filibusterers witness the dreams of success turn to ruins amidst the destruction of their hastily constructed fortress. Once again, the gentlemen from Leon and Castile had checked the eastern threat on Texas but the price was becoming increasingly higher.

The Death of Ben Milam at the Veramendi Palace in San Antonio on December 7, 1835, captures the moment of shock and disbelief in which his companions suddenly realize their gallant leader has died. Lost in a second of deafening silence amidst the roar of battle, the tired and worn-out Texans, including a field doctor, look helplessly at the man who had motivated the actual storming of San Antonio with his immortal "Who will follow old Ben to San Antone?" They had followed Ben and although they were to leave him behind, it was for him and Texas that they went on to victory.

The Signing of the Declaration of Independence on March 2, 1836 depicts the moment Collin McKinney affixed his signature to the document. Standing to his left at the right of the scene is one of the two native Texas signers, José Antonio Navarro of San Antonio. Sterling Robertson is also standing but on the right of McKinney and looking over his shoulder at the historic document. Sitting on McKinney's right in front of Robertson is James Collinsworth, his hand to his chin as he ponders a thought in conversation with Robert Potter. Over Collinsworth's shoulder is Navarro's nephew, the only other native Texan signer, José Francisco Ruiz. To his right and also standing is the learned, distinguished Lorenzo de Zavala. Thomas J. Rusk is to Zavala's right on the day that Texas became a republic.

The Annexation of Texas to the Union on February 19, 1846 captures the mixed emotions of the ceremony which formally brought the Republic of Texas to an end. While all eyes are fixed on the rising Union flag, last Texas President Anson Jones tenderly holds the flag of the Republic which crashed to the ground while being lowered. Oblivious to the crowd about him, President Jones seems lost in the reminiscing thoughts of the short-lived Republic of Texas. Standing on the podium behind Jones is James P. Henderson and behind him is R. E. B. Baylor, both engrossed in the promise that lies before them.

Sam Houston's Moment of Decision depicts that historic scene of March 16, 1861, when the old Governor, General and ex-President of Texas decided to remain loyal to the Union and advise the citizenry against joining the Confederacy. Standing behind him with her hand on his shoulder is Mrs. Houston, lending a wife's moral support to her husband. Also present at the moment are D. B. Culberson, Sam Bogart and Ben Epperson, friends of Sam Houston.

—Richard G. Santos
Archivist of Bexar County
Office of County Clerk

Acknowledgments

The publishers of this volume wish to thank the many people who have worked so hard to complete it. *Six Flags* is the fifth book in the series that began with *Heroes of Texas*. Many of our authors have written for each book. To all the authors we say thanks for their time and talent. Governor Connally has once again taken the time to write the Introduction. Joe B. Frantz took time which he could not spare to write the Foreword. The beautiful paintings reproduced here were done by Donald M. Yena, a fine artist whose feel for history is captured in every painting he does. Mr. Richard G. Santos not only wrote an article but was the historical consultant for the paintings. Miss Laura Simmons did an excellent job in reading the proofs and Mrs. Frances Haynes proved again to be the best secretary and all-around assistant any publisher ever had. Mr. Dayton Kelley was always ready to look up and check any detail that was needed. The entire staffs of Davis Bros. Publishing Co. and Library Binding Company took the raw material and produced a fine book. Travis Lawson of Advertising and Marketing Associates helped tremendously in all phases of this production. Pat Rinewalt of Olmsted-Kirk Paper Company contributed patience and time which were so important. To all these we say thank you and may we all continue to work together for many years to come.

Texian Press

Table of Contents

Rène Robert Cavelier La Salle . . . . . Page 1

Philip Nolan . . . . Page 31

The Siege and Storming of Bexar . . . . Page 57

The Texas Declaration of Independence . Page 75

From Republic to State:
        The Annexation of Texas . . . . . Page 95

Texas Joins the Confederacy . . . . . Page 113

The French

1684 - 1685

The Founding of Fort St. Louis -- March 1685

Rène Robert Cavelier La Salle

by

DORMAN H WINFREY

The first settlement of the French in Texas was but a tiny colony; harboring a hundred souls, it perched for a time on the coast of Texas, vulnerable alike to the Indians on shore and the Spanish at sea, and at last was gone as suddenly as it had appeared. Only in its prompting of what others did was it to leave a mark on the land that would one day be the Lone Star State. Yet its founders lodged within its frail ramparts the grandest visions of empire: Fort St. Louis they named it, as much for the Sun King himself as for the royal saint.

The origins of Fort St. Louis were as much a product of the man who founded it as of the nation from which its inhabitants came. Rène Robert Cavelier, Sieur de la Salle, was to become the greatest French explorer of the Mississippi Valley. Certainly he was one of the greatest explorers of any country, in an age abounding in courageous and far-sighted men seeking lands beyond the seas, and one of his followers considered him "one of the greatest men of this age." Yet at the age of forty-three he would be dead, his most magnificent scheme come to nothing and his visions of a new French empire a failure.

He was born in Rouen, France, in 1632, into a family well-to-do and well connected at court, with high diplomatic and court posts, but not of the nobility. The title Sieur de la Salle derived from the name of a family estate near Rouen, in accordance with a tradition by which the wealthy French burghers often borrowed titles for members of their families from their landed estates.

The details of La Salle's youth are few and uncertain. As a boy he received an excellent education, particularly in mathematics, for which he seems to have shown a special aptitude. He studied at the Jesuit College in Rouen, probably as a novice for the priesthood. It appears that he taught school for a time under jurisdiction of the Jesuits, but in the end his spirit rebelled against the regimentation of the religious life and he left it. It is said that he parted on good terms with the order, receiving commendation on his excellent reputation in achievements and morals.

When he dissociated himself from the Jesuits, La Salle was thrown on his own resources, for by the laws of France he had given up his rights of inheritance when he associated with the order. An allowance of three or four hundred livres a year was given him, but he was not the kind of man to rely on what providence bestowed. Instead, he sought ways of giving expression to the spirit of inquiry and adventure that were to dominate his life.

He saw his big opportunity in the lands to the west, where France had begun to establish herself in the wild reaches of Canada. There soldiers and missionaries had already made a beginning, and among those who sought to make a life among the Indians of the New World was La Salle's brother, the Abbe Jean Cavelier, a priest at the monastery of St. Sulpice at Montreal. In 1666 La Salle embarked to join his brother and to begin those excursions into the wilderness of North America where he was to meet both his fame and his downfall.

What kind of man was this La Salle, who left the safety and comforts of his native country to take up an uncertain existence in a new land? Certainly, he was courageous. Even in later years, when his reputation was maligned by attacks from those who envied or resented him, no one ever cast doubt on his willingness to undertake the most difficult and demanding tasks, that would have deterred a lesser spirit. His was that kind of character whose forcefulness demands recognition—he inspired hatred as well as respect and admiration; but no one who associated with him closely seems to have been able to remain indifferent to him. One of the most revealing evidences, perhaps, of the strength of his character was the response he was able to draw from the Indians he met in North America. Almost all those who viewed his activities in the New World noted the great respect he inspired among them—perhaps because they did not demand the refined social amenities of the European courts, but judged men on their own merits.

La Salle was a serious man, highly dedicated to what he believed in, and not given to diversions that would distract him from his purpose. His whole life he gave to the goals he set himself, and every movement, every statement almost, was devoted to them. Not for him were the casual pleasures of the court or a life of idle diversions. Almost from the beginning, his ambitions were thwarted by misfortune and opposition, but never for a moment did he allow them to discourage him from pursuing his dreams.

He was a leader, with the spirit and initiative to draw other men around him, and to persuade others of the value of what he himself believed in. But most of all, he was ambitious, a true man of his age. His was not the ambition of the merchant, grappling in the markets for gold, but his was a higher design. It has been said of him that he "was a very indifferent trader; and his heart was not in the commercial part of his enterprise. He aimed at achievement, and thirsted after greatness." He himself would later write to his government of his adventures in the new world, "Since I have been in this country, I have had neither servants nor clothes nor fare which did not savor more of meanness than of ostentation; and the moment I see that there is anything with which either you or the court find fault, I assure you that I will give it up: for the life I am leading has no other attraction for me than that of honor; and the more danger and difficulty there are in undertakings of this sort, the more worthy of honor I think they are."

An acquaintance noted his honesty: "All those among my friends who have seen him find him a man of great intelligence and sense. He rarely speaks of any subject except when questioned about it, and his words are very few and very precise. He distinguishes perfectly between that which he knows with certainty and that which he knows with some mingling of doubt. When he does not know, he does not hesitate to avow it; and though I have heard him say the same thing more than five or six times, when persons were present who had not heard it before, he always said it in the same manner. In short, I never heard anybody speak whose words carried with them more marks of truth."

But admirable though many of his personal qualities were, La Salle had certain human failings which were in the end to be his destruction, and were before that time to earn him many enemies. Chief among these were his reserved and haughty manner, and his apparent inability to respond with warmth to personal relationships. Though he had several admirers, he does not appear to have had many deep friendships.

Even those who followed him to the very end were not privy to his thoughts, for he kept to himself and seems to have had a deep-seated distrust of others. One of his staunchest admirers wrote of him, "His firmness, his courage, his great knowledge of the arts and sciences, which made him equal to every undertaking, and his untiring energy, which enabled him to surmount every obstacle, would have won at last a glorious success for his grand enterprise, had not all his fine qualities been counterbalanced by a haughtiness of manner which often made him insupportable, and by a harshness towards those under his command, which drew upon him an implacable hatred, and was at last the cause of his death." He drove his men as he drove himself, and because they were lesser men than he, they at last rebelled, and so he was destroyed.

Among his fellow men La Salle lacked that open spirit which inspires confidence and leads to support and succor. An acquaintance wrote of him that he was "serious in all things, incapable of the lighter pleasures, incapable of repose, finding no joy but in the pursuit of great designs, too shy for society and too reserved for popularity, often unsympathetic and always seeming so, smothering emotions which he could not utter, schooled to universal distrust, stern to his followers and pitiless to himself, bearing the brunt of every hardship and every danger, demanding of others an equal constancy joined to an implicit deference, heeding no counsel but his own, attempting the impossible and grasping at what was too vast to hold,—he contained in his own company and painful nature the chief springs of his triumphs, his failures, and his death." Even, evidently, when it was to his advantage to propitiate others, he could not bring himself to do it. "His enemies were numerous and vindictive, but he neither took the pains to conciliate them, nor apparently had he the tact to do so, had he tried. He was coldly ambitious, reserved to hauteur, overconfident in his own judgment, with great natural ability and equal determination, imaginative to a fault, and consequently often more visionary than practical."

No charges were ever made of him that he lacked honor or integrity; most of his detractors seemed to feel rather that he was full of "crack-brained schemes," if not actually insane; that he was harsh to his men, that he traded where he had no right to trade; and that his discoveries were but a pretense for making money. Some of these charges must be attributed to jealousy on the part of those who were less successful than he, for there is no doubt that for a time he was successful, financially and politically. Still, there seems to be a grain of truth to the accusations, particularly to the charge of adopting a scheme without fully realizing its demands and limitations. And he seems at times to have been overcome by indecision to the point of not being able to make even the most basic plans. And some present-day detractors flatly state his incompetence: "He continued Joliet's exploration from the Arkansas River to the Gulf of Mexico; then wasted two years, $50,000, and 150 lives in Texas, without being able to get beyond the Sabine or reach the Arkansas, as some of his party easily did after his death."

Above all, La Salle was a man of his time. It was an age of exploration, and he was a leading explorer; it was an age of intellectual rediscovery, and he was possessed of an insatiable curiosity; it was an age of rampant nationalism, and he was a devoted standard bearer of the banner of France. He came upon the scene at a time when the spirit of the age demanded men willing to stake their lives for ideas still unproven, and he was a man for his times.

To the seventeenth century, science was the religion, and men like Galileo, Leibnitz, Isaac Newton, and Descartes were its saints. In mathematics, physics, astronomy, anatomy, and, indeed, every branch of science, new attitudes and new discoveries were setting the stage in the intellectual world for the activities that would be taking place in the economic and political spheres. The triumph of empirical philosophy gave rise to a company of scientific societies which proliferated throughout Europe; such bodies as the Royal Society and the Royal Observatory in England and the Academie des Sciences in France won charters to pursue the dominate spirit of the age. The mind of Europe was reaching out toward the unknown, discovering the world, exploring new concepts; and it was but natural that intellectual speculation should tempt some men to test in action what was theorized in the circles of the educated, and that when temptation was reinforced by international competition for trade and empire, it became an irresistible force.

Colonial aggressiveness was one mark of the century's spirit of enterprise and inquiry. It was a period of declared and undeclared wars, as the big trading powers—France, Spain, England, and the Netherlands—competed for the newly-discovered markets and riches of the world. The dream of the age was China, and its passion was a direct route to its shores. Trade and empire were the prizes for which nations attacked each other on the sea, and raced with each other across the oceans. It was this consuming desire to acquire new lands which impelled La Salle and others like him to see the New World.

When La Salle arrived in Montreal, it was "perhaps the most dangerous place in Canada," threatened constantly by the Iroquois Indians. For the moment there was a treaty of peace with the tribe, but the settlers lived in perpetual expectation that it would be broken. The French settlement was under the practical proprietorship of the Seminary of St. Sulpice, which acted much as a corporation of priests with the feudal lordship of Montreal. The land which they had been granted by the French crown was still largely unsettled, and they were eager to attract settlers. For this reason they were offering very easy terms to settlers in hopes of establishing a line of settlements along the front of their island to form an outpost from which an alarm could be given in the event of the Iroquois' attacking. La Salle arrived in time to take advantage of this situation.

He received from Queylus, the Superior of the Seminary, a large tract of land eight or nine miles from Montreal, later to be called La Chine. The land, situated as it was away from the main settlement, was greatly exposed to Indian attack, but it was also very favorably located for the fur trade on which the French in Canada depended.

Over this land, La Salle became a sort of feudal proprietor, and immediately began to improve it and make grants to settlers. At the same time, he began to prepare himself for the explorations he would undertake in the New World; he began a study of the Indian languages, and it was said that within two or three years he mastered the Iroquois and seven or eight other languages and dialects.

La Salle spent two years in this manner, setting up his colony, building a fort for defense, and encouraging immigrants to settle there. He also encouraged the growth of trade, constructing vessels to move the furs handled through his colony onto Lake Ontario and to the sea. By the end of two years, he was said to have been earning an annual income of 25,000 livres.

Between his arrival and 1683 La Salle carried on a series of Mississippi explorations, which extended the domain of the French in North America. Prior to 1670 he had explored the Illinois and Ohio Rivers, descending the latter as far as Louisville. By 1683 he had built the first sailing vessel on Lake Erie and erected Fort Miami on the St. Joseph and Forts Crevecoeur and St. Louis on the Illinois.

Fort St. Louis became his headquarters and the strongest French bulwark against the Iroquois. These fierce fighters were dreaded not only by the white settlers, but by their neighbor Indians, and the fort soon became a haven for all those who feared them. Nearly 4,000 warriors gathered at the fort as allies of the white men against the Iroquois, and a village of nearly 300 dwellings grew up about the fort. To Fort St. Louis, also, the western tribes brought their furs, to be traded with the French for trinkets and hunting weapons; and so the fort became a center of the fur trade.

Like all the early explorers, La Salle was impelled by the dream of a passage west to the South Sea and the wealth of the East. One winter, while at Fort St. Louis, he was visited by a band of Seneca Iroquois who told him of a river they called the Ohio rising in their country and flowing into the sea, but at such a distance that its mouth could be reached only after a journey of eight or nine months. This "Great River," La Salle concluded, was the long-awaited route to the East; and from that moment his eagerness to journey to its mouth dominated his thoughts.

Inspired by the tale of the "Great River," La Salle contracted to build two vessels to sail down the Mississippi to its mouth; by 1681 he had attempted this venture twice, and finally abandoned it as impracticable, deciding instead in favor of a journey by foot and canoe. In December, 1681, he embarked on the final voyage that was to bring him success. By April of the following year he had reached the mouth of the river, and on April 9, 1826, he claimed possession in the name of France, "of this country of Louisiana, the seas, harbors, ports, bays, adjacent straits, and all the nations, people, provinces, cities, towns, villages, mines, minerals, fisheries, streams and rivers comprised in the extent of said Louisiana, from the mouth of the great river St. Louis on the eastern side . . . as far as its mouth at the sea, or Gulf of Mexico. . . ." With his arrival at the mouth of the Mississippi, La Salle realized that the river did not give a direct outlet to the Vermilion Sea, or Gulf of California, as he had hoped. Still, it offered a means of communication from the Gulf of Mexico to the French settlements in Canada, and a shorter route to the western half of the continent than did a route from Canada. To gain control of its territory, therefore, he soon formed the plan of establishing a colony on the Gulf and a series of outposts between that colony and Canada.

La Salle had insinuated himself in the good graces of the governor of French Canada, Louis de Buade Frontenac at Palluau, and by his support had been enabled to undertake many of his ventures. In 1674, bearing with him the recommendations of the governor, La Salle returned to France, there to petition for a patent of nobility and for a grant of seignory of Fort Frontenac, a new outpost, which Governor Frontenac had constructed on his own initiative. When he returned to Canada, La Salle's prospects were at their height; he was the practical ruler of the settlements of the lands and islands around Fort Frontenac and he was almost sole profiteer of the fur trade carried on through the forts he had founded.

In 1677 La Salle, bearing with him the recommendations of the governor, again visited France to seek further privileges and financial assistance in extending his explorations and the fur trade westward, together with the permission to build forts. He was rewarded with authority to carry on exploration in the Mississippi Valley and to hold a monopoly of the fur trade there. It was these assurances of support from the crown that enabled him to carry out his expedition to the mouth of the Mississippi, but in 1683 an event occurred which was to give the death blow to his efforts in La Nouvelle France, French Canada.

In that year, Governor Frontenac was recalled to France, and was replaced by Le Febvre de la Barre, an ally of a party of merchants that had grown up in opposition to La Salle. La Salle made overtures to the new governor, but to no avail. La Barre seized Forts Frontenac and St. Louis, on the grounds that La Salle had not maintained a sufficient garrison and had not fulfilled the conditions of his grant. He then ordered

La Salle to report to Quebec; but La Salle, seeing what his future would be if he followed that course, ignored the order and departed for France to seek redress at court.

In France, La Salle was still in favor by reason of his successes in establishing trade and forts in the New World; furthermore, he arrived at a time when the government was embroiled with Spain in a struggle for empire, and his arrival soon came to be viewed as a new opportunity to frustrate the Spanish. Spain had forbidden French ships to enter the Gulf of Mexico under threat of capture or destruction, and France, to offset the virtual monopoly of Spain in the Gulf, wished to establish a port there as a permanent menace to Spanish colonies in Mexico and to treasure ships sailing in the Gulf, and as a basis for future conquest in the Spanish provinces of northern Mexico.

In the early seventeenth century the Spanish Empire was the only existing colonial empire, most of which was accrued when it acquired the Portuguese Empire. No other European nation had succeeded in founding overseas colonies. But this was soon to change; Spain had already reached the apex of its strength, and the other nations of Europe were poised to seize what should be left in the wake of her departure from the center of power. Among these nations France stood foremost; and Louis XIV, confusing national aspirations with personal ambition, was already scheming to topple the weakening power of Spain and seize its empire when in 1684 La Salle approached him with a plan which promised an additional opportunity to harass the Spanish.

La Salle, for his part, continued to dream of new explorations and new settlements. It was his belief that an ideal location for a colony would be at the mouth of the Mississippi, which would give France not only a port on the Gulf, but a shorter access to the lands in the west than the route from Canada. Even while still in Canada he had written to a friend that he planned to "pursue by sea the plans I have begun here by land," and that he ought to abandon the difficult access to the Gulf through Canada and open a route to the western areas through the Gulf and the Mississippi. It was this plan which he now brought, with certain modifications to suit the political climate, before the court.

The motives which were finally to bring La Salle to the land of Texas were, thus, in part an extension of French foreign policy, and in part a product of the personal aspirations of the explorer himself. In order to execute his plans, La Salle presented to the court two memorials, in which his own desires were hidden under an argument appealing to the ambitions of national policy. The first memorial proposed to return to Louisia ia by way of the Gulf of Mexico and the mouth of the Mississippi, and requested for the purpose one vessel and 200 men, with arms, ammunition, pay, and maintenance. The second proposed a location for the construction of a fort on the River Colbert, as he diplomatically called the Mississippi, sixty leagues above its mouth, and further proposed to undertake a conquest of New Biscay, the northern province of Spanish Mexico. His purpose, said the memorial, was "to satisfy the wish expressed to him by the late Monseigneur Colbert of finding a port where the French might establish themselves and harass the Spaniard in those regions from whence they derive all their wealth."

The memorial then presented the manner in which La Salle should accomplish this feat; and to those at the court, who had no conception of what the new world was like and who had, in any case, a great desire to wish it true, the argument sounded convincing.

In fact, it was almost ludicrous; and one wonders if La Salle himself, carried away by what he hoped could be, actually believed it possible, or whether he was merely presenting a strong argument, knowing that only a portion of what he presented could ever be realized. Whatever the case, he made the expedition sound like a carefully planned one. "There never was," he wrote, "an enterprise of such great importance proposed at so little risk and expense. . . ."

He would, he wrote, leave France with two hundred men, and from that point his argument grew less and less capable of substantiation. "Fifty more men," he said, "will join him who are in the country, and fifty buccaneers can be taken in passing at St. Domingo. The savages who are at Fort St. Louis, to the number of more than four thousand warriors, together with many others who will join, can be directed to descend the river." He then presented a detailed plan of attack on the Spanish province of northern Mexico. "It would not," he concluded, "require much time to bring this expedition to an end, since it is nearly certain that the savages can be assembled next winter and complete this conquest in the spring, in sufficient time to report the news of it by the time the first vessel returns to France." Whether because of supreme confidence, or because Louis XIV was too shrewd to endorse the scheme without assurance, La Salle agreed to repay all costs to the crown or forfeit the government of any ports established by him if execution of his project was prevented by peace with Spain for more than three years. Such were his magnificent plans.

No doubt much of La Salle's misplaced confidence in the success of his venture was a result of misinformation. The area, for instance, now known as Texas was almost entirely suppressed from the map on which he based his plans. Nevertheless, that some of his proposals were destined to failure should have been obvious to La Salle, even with his scanty knowledge. The impracticabilities of his plan were almost innumerable; the 4,000 Indians which he planned to bring down from Fort St. Louis would have to cover 2,000 miles, a journey for which they could not possibly muster sufficient canoes or provisions. Furthermore, of the total 15,000 Indians he proposed to use as allies against the Spanish, some were hostile to the French and to each other. These factors, however, La Salle carefully neglected to mention in his memorial. That he was able to gain acceptance for the plan was due in part no doubt to the ignorance of those to whom it was addressed about the country he would be in, and in part to the intensity of their wish to believe it possible.

His proposition was, however, accepted, and preparations were begun in 1684 for the journey to the Gulf. He was allowed four ships. The flagship was *Le Joly*, a man-of-war of the Royal Navy bearing thirty-six or forty guns; and in addition there were a frigate, the *Belle*, of six guns which was given by the king; a flyboat, the *Amiable*, on which were to be carried provisions for the new settlement; and the ketch *St. Francis*, bearing thirty tons of ammunition and some supplies to be delivered to the colony on Santo Domingo. A total of 280 persons were to embark on the voyage, including the crews of the ships and 100 soldiers; the remainder included mechanics, laborers, thirty volunteers, several families and girls hoping to marry and settle in the new world, and missionaries. The last included La Salle's brother Abbe Jean, who had accompanied La Salle from Canada. The quality of the new settlers left much to be desired; the soldiers who were to protect them and engage the Spanish in Mexico were described as "mere wretched beggars soliciting alms, many too, deformed and unable to fire a musket." And later when they had arrived at their landing, the colonists were to discover that their carpenters were incapable even of furnishing them suitable shelters.

From the very beginning the company was plagued by adversities. La Salle himself seems to have been stricken by one of his periodic attacks of indecision, and talked one day of going to Canada, and the next of sailing for the Gulf. Possibly he did this as a deliberate effort to misguide the Spanish of his intentions; yet its chief result was to antagonize even his faithful followers. He was highly suspicious and doubted the integrity and loyalty of his men, so that even before they sailed ill feeling and dissension plagued the party. It was to continue to the very end of the expedition.

The chief cause of discord was the breakdown of relations between La Salle and Captain de Beaujeu, who had been placed in charge of the ships during the voyage until the troops were landed. Beaujeu resented being under the command of a civilian, while La Salle suspected Beaujeu of acting as a spy on his activities. Those who supported La Salle and later wrote of the expedition placed, rather unfairly, the whole cause of the expedition's failure in the hands of Beaujeu. Yet, La Salle was not without blame. Beaujeu appears to have been a dedicated professional officer who, although he bombarded the minister of marine with complaints and requests to share the command, still seems to have determined to accept and make the best of a bad situation. "I shall go straight forward," he wrote, "without regarding a thousand whims and *bagatelles*. His [La Salle's] continual suspicion would drive anybody mad except a Norman like me; but I shall humor him, as I have always done, even to sailing my ship on dry land if he likes." La Salle, for his part, did nothing to conciliate his master of the fleet, but continued to ignore his justified attempts to determine the course and nature of the expedition. He drew up a long list of articles, defining the respective rights and functions of the two men, and demanded that Beaujeu sign it. Beaujeu refused to do so, saying that the articles gave so many military honors to La Salle that "if a marshal of France should come on board his ship, he would have none left to offer him." Finally, the terms of the document were modified and Beanjeu consented to set his name to it.

At last, dissension suppressed though not settled, the fleet weighed anchor for the voyage across the sea. On July 24, 1684, the four ships sailed from Rochelle. Almost immediately one of those incidents occurred which were to mar the expedition throughout. Only four days after sailing, the *Joly* broke her bowsprit, and the voyagers were forced to turn back into port for repairs. La Salle's suspicious nature immediately conjured up plots of sabotage, but the damage was restored and the voyage resumed.

The trip across the Atlantic was beset with the usual hardships of an ocean voyage in the tiny ships of the day, but was otherwise without mishap, and at last, after two months they approached the island of Santo Domingo, where they were to deliver supplies for the colony there. A council had been held of the officers of the expedition, at which it had been decided to stop at Port de Paix. And that was the source of the first major mistake of the expedition.

Instead of steering to Port de Paix as had been planned, the *Joly,* outdistancing her slower sister ships, ran past it in the night and anchored on the south side of the island at Petit Goave. La Salle and those who closely supported him accused Beaujeu of deliberately ignoring the orders to land at Port de Paix, but it is possible, since it was night and a storm had come up and dispersed the ships, that he had merely gone there as a place of refuge. That is, in fact, what the *Amiable* and the *Belle* did, and on the fourteenth of September, 1684, they joined the *Joly* in port there.

When the *Joly* landed at Petit Goave, she had on board fifty men who were ill, including La Salle, who was moved on shore to recover. Soon it was learned that the unarmed ketch *St. Francis* had put into Port de Paix to escape the storm, and after it subsided had sailed to join the other ships. Caught off guard by two Spanish ships, she had been captured with all her stores and ammunition. This blow to the expedition, as well as the necessity of giving the sick time to recover and refurnishing the supplies, kept the three remaining ships in port until the last part of November.

The Abbe Jean reported in his journal of the expedition that "M. de Beaujeu began to employ all means that the could invent to prevent my brother from going further." Nevertheless, on November 28 the ships departed to reconnoitre the coast line in search of the mouth of the Mississippi, La Salle changing his own quarters from the *Joly* to the *Amiable*.

Leaving Santo Domingo, they took a course along the Cayman Islands, anchored a day at the Isle of Pines to take in water, then continued to Port San Antonio on the island of Cuba, where they found that the Spanish had abandoned some provisions and wine, which they took. After two days' delay caused by bad weather they left Cuba and continued into the Gulf of Mexico. From that point the expedition floundered, at the mercy of its ignorance and the pettiness of its members. No one of the party knew anything of the navigation of the Gulf; they did know, however, that the Spanish patrolled the Gulf and that they had threatened extermination to any French caught in its waters. In Santo Domingo the voyagers had attempted to acquire information that would guide them through the unfamiliar waterway; and the advice they received was to betray them totally. La Salle had there been led to believe that the Gulf stream ran more strongly than was actually the case, and so he overestimated his distance traveled. Furthermore, although from his discovery two years previously La Salle knew the latitude of the river, he did not know its longitude.

On the twenty-fifth of December, after following a northwesterly course, the ships sighted land. By December 27 La Salle was probably within fifty miles of the mouth of the Mississippi's main channel, when he changed his course to west-northwest; this misjudgment was to cost him his chance of success. On New Year's Day, 1685, the ships anchored offshore, probably by present Jefferson County, while La Salle went on shore to investigate the territory.

Two days later there was a thick fog over the area and when it cleared the *Joly* had disappeared—said the Abbe Jean later, "under pretext of having been surprised by a squall." On January 9 the sailors spied a wide opening between two low points of land where the adjacent sea was discolored with mud; this, they assumed, must be the Mississippi. Actually it was probably the entrance to Galveston Bay; they did not stop to examine it, however, because of the objections of the pilot of the *Amiable* and the need to keep a watch for the *Joly.* Continuing west southwest, La Salle made several unsuccessful attempts to land men on shore, but was repelled by sand bars and breakers. At last on January 17 he succeeded in landing a boat, probably near Mad Island Slough in southwestern Matagorda County. Here his men looked in vain for fresh water and shot some ducks and geese, then returned to the *Amiable.*

Resuming their course southwest, the ships made several trips to scout the coast. On the nineteenth, the fog lifted to reveal the *Joly* approaching from the distance. Then followed a council in which Beanjeu and La Salle exchanged mutual accusations on causing the separation and debated the position of the fleet. They did not realize it, but they had sailed over 400 miles west of the mouth of the Mississippi.

In need of water and provisions, La Salle determined to return to the area of his previous landing and search by land for a site which would offer a temporary settlement place and safe harbor for the ships. On January 20, a camp was established, probably "about four miles inland on Buttermilk Slough, a tributary of Turtle Bay in the present southwestern Matagorda County." Here La Salle in all likelihood first determined with certainty that he had passed the mouth of the Mississippi. Men were sent ashore to travel west, while the ships followed them along the coast, and ordered to signal when a suitable site was located. Arriving at Lavaca Bay, they signaled the ships, and La Salle joined them.

Deciding that the bay offered a haven for his ships, La Salle ordered the captains to enter a pass, probably present-day Pass Cavallo, and anchor within the bay. After taking soundings to determine the depth of the channel and setting stakes to mark the course of the ships, the captains were told to proceed "cautiously under short sail at high tide."

Instead, the captain of the *Amiable* set full sail and sped into the pass. As the ship moved into the channel, La Salle was on shore watching, while a party of his men were a short distance away cutting down a tree to make a canoe. Suddenly a group of them ran toward him calling out that they had been attacked by a troop of Indians, who had seized the rest of the party and carried them off. La Salle ordered his men on shore to take their weapons and he immediately set off in pursuit of the

Indians. As he departed after them, he turned to look at the *Amiable*. She was just then nearing the shoals, and La Salle remarked that "if she held that course she would soon be aground."

But the press of the moment called him elsewhere, and he abandoned the ship to the incompetence or duplicity of the crew and marched to the camp of the Indians. While he was there, bargaining for the return of his men, the roar of the *Amiable's* cannon shattered the stillness of the woods, and La Salle knew that his prediction was come true. The *Amiable* had grounded.

After the wreck of the *Amiable*, the party encamped on the sand at the west side of the inlet. They tried to save as much as possible of the vessel's cargo, and did manage to salvage some gunpowder and flour, but a storm blew up and most of it was lost. Conditions were very bad, and every one was sick with nausea and dysentery; one of the survivors reported later that five or six people died every day because of the bad food and brackish water. Their rations were "flour saved from the wreck, boiled into messes of porridge, with this brackish water."

A temporary kind of protective fortification was built around the camp from wood salvaged from the wreck and uprooted trees and rotten logs washed up by the sea. "Here," wrote a chronicler of the expedition, "among tents and hovels, bales, boxes, casks, spars, dismounted cannon, and pens for fowl and swine, were gathered the dejected men and homesick women who were to seize New Biscay, and hold for France a region large as half of Europe."

Almost immediately an antagonistic relationship with the surrounding Indians was established. Some blankets left from the wreck of the *Amiable* had been left unguarded and were taken by the Indians; a party was sent out to recover them, and although the Indians gave them up without protest, they attacked the returning men, killing two of them. And later, the Indians started a fire on the prairie so that the wind would carry it to the fort; this disaster was averted when La Salle ordered all the grass cut, especially around the gunpowder.

After the establishment of the camp, to which Beaujeu refused to bring his ship into the bay for risk of the shallow water, dangerous reefs, and swift currents, the captain of the *Joly* made plans to return to France. He considered, he said, that he had accomplished his part of the assignment in landing "his passengers at what La Salle assured him to be one of the mouths of the Mississippi." By this time, his relations with La Salle had improved somewhat; he wrote La Salle two days before the wreck, "I wish with all my heart that you would have more confidence in me. For my part, I will always make the first advances; and I will follow your counsel whenever I can do so without risking my ship. I will come back to this place, if you want to know the results of the voyage I am going to make. If you wish, I will go to Martinique for provisions and reinforcements. In fine, there is nothing I am not ready to do; you have only to speak."

For some reason, La Salle turned down Beaujeu's offer to bring back supplies, but requested that he bring up from the hold of his ship the cannon and iron that had been stored there for the colony. After fulfilling this request, Beaujeu set sail on March 12 to go to Mobile Bay to get food, water, and other supplies for his ships before returning to France. He took with him some of the would-be colonists, as well as Minet, the engineer, who on his return to the homeland was arrested for deserting La Salle.

After Beaujeu left, the party built storehouses on shore for ammunition and provisions, and looked for a more permanent settlement place. It had quickly become evident that the camp site was unsuitable for residence, and with spring La Salle set out to explore the area. He was resolved to continue his quest for the Mississippi, as soon as he could locate the settlers on a better site. While on his trip he located a suitable place on a small hill about five miles up the Lavaca River, and there he proposed to move all the women and children in the company and most of the men, while Henri Joutel and about thirty men were left at the camp to prepare wood to be used in building a fort.

Joutel was a careful observer and it is through his journal that we have our best idea of what life was like for those who followed La Salle. According to his account, with their numbers diminished, life became easier for those left at the camp, for they could provide for their own diminished needs by hunting and fishing, so that, said Joutel, "we lived well enough contented. . . ."

Ingenuity made their life easier; they soon discovered that nature offered much to those who were perceptive enough to recognize her gifts. Their discovery of a salt supply was typical of how they learned to live from the land. "Providence also showed us," wrote Joutel, "that there was salt, made by the sun, upon several little salt water pools there were in divers places, for, having observed that these grew on them a sort of white substance, like the cream upon milk, I took care every day to send and fetch that scum off, which proved to be as very white and good salt, whereof I gathered a quantity, and it did us good service."

Soon, however, the undercurrent of discontent that had rankled among the settlers from the beginning threatened to break into the open. Two men deserted, and some others attempted to escape, but were caught and one was hanged as an example. Then Joutel discovered a plot afoot to kill himself and another loyal follower of La Salle; though Joutel suppressed it, it brought to the surface the smoldering animosities that La Salle had been able to hold in check. And Joutel was beset in addition with fears of the Indians and of discovery by the Spanish. A Spanish ship did in fact pass down the Gulf, but did not notice the camp.

By midsummer Joutel and his men had gathered a sufficient supply of building materials to bring to the construction site, and they were ordered to join the main body of the settlers, while the *Belle* was towed up the bay to join them.

The precise location of the fort is still a matter of dispute. E. W. Cole places it at Dimmitt's Point on the Lavaca River in Jackson County, while H. E. Bolton placed it on Garcitas Creek in Victoria County. The new fort was titled Fort St. Louis. Some wood was brought for its construction from Joutel's camp, but much of it had to be felled and brought in from a distance. There was no wood within a league of the building site and no horses or oxen to drag it. The carpenters brought from Rochelle proved worthless; La Salle himself made the plans of the work and directed construction. All were put to work; "some felled and squared the timber; and others dragged it by main force over the matted grass of the prairie under the scorching Texas sun," and the strenuous labor took its toll among the lives and health of the colonists.

The fort itself consisted of a large timber building, roofed with boards and raw hides, divided into apartments for lodging and other uses. The colonists had sown crops, but by the time Joutel had joined them, drought had destroyed most of the plants.

On moving into the new fort, La Salle felt it necessary for the safety of the colonists to arrive at some kind of solution to the problem of the Indians living in the vicinity of the fort, whom Joutel called "that crafty nation." Father Le Clercq, who accompanied La Salle during most of his travels in Texas, wrote that "On the 13th of October, the Sieur de la Salle, seeing himself constantly insulted by the savages, and wishing, moreover, to have some of their canoes, by force or consent, as he could not do without them, resolved to make open war on them in order to bring them to an advantageous peace." In this he was successful for the moment, for he drove off the Indians, permitting the colonists to build houses and sow fields of grain; in the long run, however, the hatred inspired by this act was to result in the destruction of the fort and its inhabitants.

By July, 1685, the fort was completed and La Salle renewed his preparations for seeking the "fatal river." From October, 1685, to March,

1686, he spent his time exploring the surrounding territory, probably hoping to find the elusive Mississippi, but perhaps also trying to locate Spanish settlements. The exact routes he took are disputed, but evidently he explored west of the fort as well as to the east.

La Salle made a series of explorations during which he found evidence that the Spanish had already established a transient site of some sort about fifteen leagues from Fort St. Louis. His brother's later report told of reaching "a large village, enclosed with a kind of wall of clay and sand, and fortified with little towers at intervals, where he found the arms of Spain engraved on a plate of copper, with the date of 1588, attached to a stake. The inhabitants gave us a kind welcome, and showed us some hammers and an anvil, two small pieces of iron cannon, a small brass culverin, some pike-heads, sword-blades, and some books of Spanish comedy; and thence they guided us to a little hamlet of fishermen, about two leagues distant, where they showed us a second stake, also with the arms of Spain, and a few old chimneys. All this convinced us that the Spaniards had formerly been here."

On the last day of October, 1685, La Salle set out to find the Mississippi. It was his first major expedition from Fort St. Louis, for which, wrote Father Anastasius Douay, who accompanied him, "we made no preparation but four pounds of powder and four of lead, two axes, two dozen knives, as many awls, some beads and two kettles." With him went fifty men.

Joutel was left in charge of the fort, and it is his journal that provides our best picture of the life at Fort St. Louis. While the commander was gone, Joutel attempted to pull together the spirits of the little community. La Salle had, he thought, by his own serious and single-minded devotion to finding the Mississippi, oppressed the mood of the people, and he attempted in his chief's absence to restore their energies. He tried to keep everyone busy, that their minds would not dwell on their hardships; and to this end he had constructed new separate lodgings for the women and girls, a chapel, and a defensive palisade. About the four corners of the latter he set eight pieces of cannon; these, however, were less effective than they might have been; for there were no balls for them; instead, they were loaded with bags of bullets. In addition Joutel had built an oven and a rack on which buffalo meat could be dried, which contributed greatly to the welfare of the fort's inhabitants.

Food for the settlement was plentiful, and this aided in maintaining its spirits. In addition to some hogs and chickens brought from France, there was an abundance of wildlife in the neighboring marshes and waters. Joutel reported that the settlers found not only fish, oysters, and turtles, but on the prairies buffalo, deer, hare, turkeys, ducks, geese, and numerous other wild fowl.

Joutel throughout his journal exhibited a strong interest in the native fauna and flora of the new world, and was particularly struck by what he considered the bizarre forms which the native animals took. Rattlesnakes and alligators especially fascinated him, probably because they had made victims of the settlers and their livestock. Of the latter he wrote, "there are also many alligators in the rivers, some of them of a frightful magnitude and bulk. I killed one that was between four and five foot about and twenty feet in length, on which our swine feasted. This creature had very short legs, insomuch that it rather drags along than walks, and it is easy to follow the track of it, either among the weeds or on the sands, where it has been. It is very ravenous, and attacks either men or beasts, when they are within reach in the river, and comes also ashore to seek for food. It has this particular quality that it flies from such as pursue and pursues those who fly from it. I have shot many of them dead."

Expounding on the rattlesnake he wrote, "Among the venomous sorts of snakes, as vipers, asps and others, whereof there are many, those called rattlesnakes are the most common. They generally lie among the brambles, where they make a noise by the motion of two scales they have at the end of their tail, which is heard at a considerable distance, and therefore they are called rattlesnakes. Some of our men had eaten of them and found their flesh was not amiss, and when we had killed any of them our swine made a good meal." Another creature that he put in the same class was the "horned frog," whose frightful appearance deceived him into thinking that it was venomous.

He also noticed "some creatures as big as an indifferent cat, very like a rat, having a bag under their throat, in which they carry their young. They feed upon nuts and acorns, are very fat, and their flesh is much like pig."

In the middle of January, a guard reported to Joutel that he had heard from the river a voice calling out, "Dominic." This was the name of the younger of two brothers named Duhaut; and when Joutel went to investigate he found the older brother, who had left with La Salle, hailing the fort from a canoe. La Salle had given Joutel strict orders not to permit anyone from the exploring party to return to rejoin the settlers, but Duhaut's story was so convincing that Joutel made an exception for him. He was later to regret his generosity.

Duhaut reported to the eager company that as La Salle and his men marched along the prairie, Duhaut, bringing up the rear, had stopped to mend his moccasin, and when he tried to overtake his companions, he mistook a buffalo trail for theirs and lost his way. At night he fired his gun as a signal to them, but received no answer. He then decided to return to the fort; locating a canoe hidden by La Salle, he paddled at night, and hid during the day in case of unfriendly Indians. For sustenance he shot turkeys, deer, and buffalo, which, because he had no knife, he was compelled to cut with a flint. Duhaut further told of the loss of the pilot of the *Belle* and five of the party to Indians. They had been ordered by La Salle to sound along the shore, and to return to their ship before nightfall. But instead, the captain and six of his men left their canoe and arms on the sand and advanced up the beach to bivouac for the night. Here they fell asleep and were surprised by an Indian party, who killed them all; La Salle, at last alarmed by their long absence, set a search for them and found their bodies. The ship was never seen again; in March it capsized on the opposite side of the bay, leaving only six survivors.

At the end of March, Joutel had mounted the roof of one of the buildings, when he saw a small group of men approaching the fort. He gathered a number of his men, and with arms ready they went out to investigate the intruders. To their delight they found La Salle returning from his exploration. He told of encounters with Indians and of yet another disappointment in coming across a large river which he at first took to be the Mississippi. He seems at that time to have still entertained plans of carrying through his original scheme of attacking the Spanish provinces; for he told also of encountering Indians who hated the Spanish and would be eager to join the French in an attack on them.

Yet it was becoming more and more obvious that the fort was growing ever weaker and increasingly less capable of sustaining itself, much less of invading Mexico. The loss of the *Belle* was a fatal blow to their hopes, for La Salle had relied on it to carry the colonists to the Mississippi when he should locate it, and had for security put on board it his papers and personal belongings, as well as large quantities of stores, ammunition, and tools. Upon his return he set men searching for her, but to no avail.

An additional blow came soon after his return, when he fell dangerously ill. He determined that as soon as he recovered he should make his way to Canada to bring back relief to the colonists and send word to France of their condition. His plan was, however, to go there by way of the Mississippi and Illinois Rivers, when he did not yet know where the Mississippi was. By the twenty-second of April, 1686, he was recovered and plans were completed for the journey. With twenty men crudely clad in what they could peace together of hides and the little available clothing, and weapons, kettles, and axes, he set out for the distant French settlements.

Again Joutel was left in charge of the fort, this time to receive confirmation of the worst fears of the settlers—that the *Belle* was lost to them. On the first of May six wretched souls arrived at the fort, the survivors of the ship, which had wrecked on the opposite side of the bay. With this news, the settlers could only place all their remaining hopes on the success of La Salle's journey. But this, too, was not to be realized. His second trip ended as had the first; of the twenty who had left the fort, only eight returned; four had deserted; one was lost; and the remainder, exhausted by the march, had probably tried to return to the fort, and had perished in the attempt. Again La Salle had learned of his Spanish predecessors; he met Comanches returning from raids on the Mexican border, and bought five horses of Spanish descent from the Cenis Indians for the sum of thirty knives, ten hatchets, and six dozen needles. While with the Indians La Salle and his nephew Moranget had been attacked by fever, and by the time they recovered their ammunition was so low that they saw their only chance would be to return to the fort.

With La Salle's return, the situation of the settlers reverted to what it had been before his departure; and again, there seemed no choice but to make another attempt to reach Canada. On this trip La Salle decided to take Joutel, and when they reached Canada, send him and Abbe Jean to France to report on the colony, while La Salle himself returned to the fort with aid. Before the trip could begin, La Salle was prostrated by an attack of hernia, from which he had long suffered; but at last the party was ready.

In January of 1687 began La Salle's last journey to reach Canada. Seventeen men left the fort, taking with them the colony's five horses to carry their supplies. Before they left, a general meeting of the whole settlement was held at which La Salle made an address, and all parted with such emotion as if they instinctively realized that this was to be their last glimpse of each other.

The expedition took a northerly course, en route hearing again from the Indians they passed of the Spanish who had preceded them, and by the fifteenth of March they were encamped within a few miles of a site which La Salle had passed on his last trip and where he had cached some Indian beans and corn. This location is given variously as near Navasota in Grimes County and near Larrison Creek in Cherokee County.

Wherever the precise location, La Salle detailed a party to locate and bring back the food supply. Sent to find it were Duhaut the elder, Liotot,

Hiens, a former buccaneer, Teissier, l'Archeveque, Nika, a Shawnee Indian hunter who had accompanied La Salle from Canada to France and then to Texas, and La Salle's personal servant, Saget. They found the contents of the hidden stores spoiled and unfit for food, but while returning empty-handed, they spied two buffalo which they shot. They then paused to dress the meat, sending the servant Saget to La Salle to inform him of the new food and to ask him to send horses to carry the meat.

On learning of this good news, La Salle immediately sent his nephew Moranget and another man named De Marle with horses to the hunters' camp. There they found Duhaut and the others had already cut up the meat, and laid it upon scaffolds for smoking. They had also put aside for themselves marrow-bones and some parts of the meat to which, by custom, they were entitled. Moranget, whether from the stress of the march or personal animosity, was outraged at this, and his lack of wisdom in handling the situation was to destroy all hopes of the expedition and end his brother's life. He seized all of the meat, and threatened to punish Duhaut and the other members of the party. This fanned into open flames the sparks of resentment that Duahaut and the surgeon, Liotot, had harbored against Moranget and La Salle; and the two persuaded the others to revenge themselves on Moranget that night. In addition, Nika and Saget were to be killed for the personal loyalty they displayed toward La Salle.

That night, Moranget, Saget, and Nika were assigned the first three guards, so that after the last had performed his duty, all three were asleep. Then, while Duhaut and Hiens stood with guns cocked, to shoot the destined victims if they attempted to resist or flee, the surgeon, with an ax, struck each sleeper a blow. Saget and Nika died instantly, but Moranget "started spasmodically into a sitting posture, gasping and unable to speak; and the murderers compelled De Marle, who was not in their plot, to compromise himself by despatching him." It did not take the murderers long to realize that, having killed the nephew of La Salle and two of his most trusted men, they would not be safe so long as the commander himself was alive. And with that realization, La Salle's fate was sealed.

La Salle, meanwhile, expecting Moranget and his companions to return shortly, waited all day, until on the eighteenth of March, he decided that he himself would set out to find them, taking Joutel with him. Joutel wrote that La Salle "became very anxious," and not knowing himself where the camp was, told some Indians in the area that he would give a hatchet to any who would guide them, and one accepted the offer.

"That evening," wrote Joutel, "while we were talking about what could have happened to the absent men, he seemed to have a presentiment of what was to take place. He asked me if I had heard any machinations of what was to take place. I answered that I had heard nothing, except that they sometimes complained of being found fault with so often; and that this was all I knew, besides which, as they were persuaded that I was in his interest, they would not have told me of any bad design they might have. We were very uneasy all the rest of the evening."

The next morning La Salle set out with the Indian guide and the friar Anastase Douay. He had changed his mind about Joutel's accompanying him, and left him in camp. The friar later described the events that befell La Salle. "All the way," he wrote, "he spoke to me of nothing but matters of piety, grace, and predestination, enlarging on the debt he owed to God, who had saved him from so many perils during more than twenty years of travel in America. Suddenly, I saw him overwhelmed with a profound sadness, for which he himself could not account. He was so much moved that I scarcely knew him." This momentary emotion passed, however, and they continued on. Soon they approached the camp on the farther side of a small river, and as they advanced toward it, La Salle noticed two birds circling in the air, "as if attracted by carcasses of beasts or men." He fired his gun and pistol as a signal to his followers if they were within hearing.

They were, but the response was not what he sought. Instead of joining him or answering his signal, they moved upstream from where he was, and there crossed the river, the trees and bushes hiding them from his sight. Duhaut and the surgeon crouched in some long grass, while l'Archeveque stepped into sight near the river bank. La Salle, seeing him, called out, demanding to know where Moranget was. To this, according to Father Douay, l'Archeveque "without lifting his hat, or any show of respect, replied in an agitated and broken voice, with a tone of studied insolence, that he was strolling about somewhere. La Salle rebuked and menaced him; he answered with increased insolence, drawing back, as he spoke, towards the ambuscade, while the incensed commander advanced to chastise him. At that moment, a shot was fired from the grass, instantly followed by another; and pierced through the brain, La Salle dropped dead."

The friar stood terror-stricken, "unable to advance or to fly," when Duhaut, rising from the ambush, called out to him that he had nothing to fear. The murderers came forward and, abusing and insulting the corpse, stripped it naked, and dragged it into some bushes, to be left for the wolves and buzzards.

After the killing of La Salle, all the men returned to the main camp, where, according to Joutel, "Father Anastase Douay . . . aghast with grief and terror, rushed into the hut of Cavelier. 'My poor brother is dead!' cried the priest, instantly divining the catastrophe from the horror-stricken face of the messenger." When they arrived, Joutel was absent, and l'Archeveque, who was not entirely in sympathy with the murderers, went to warn him of the events that had taken place. He found him on a small hill making a fire to guide La Salle back. Joutel, like the rest, expected at first a general slaughter, but l'Archeveque persuaded him that no more killing was intended if no resistance were offered, and with this reassurance Joutel returned to face the slayers of his leader and friend.

Those now in charge determined to retrace their steps to the fort on the Lavaca, for the crime that they had committed prevented their ever being safe if they returned to French territory. They at first took away the weapons of the remainder of the party, but were soon forced to return them when they realized that the others were needed to stand guard.

According to their plan, the troop set out for the shores of Lavaca Bay; en route they arrived at an Indian village, where they found two Frenchmen, former members of La Salle's group who had deserted him on the last attempt to reach Canada and were now living as Indians. Here they stayed for some time, until further dissension sent them on separate paths. Duhaut and Liotot changed their minds about returning to Fort St. Louis. Hiens, however, was determined to do so, and in order to seize control of the group himself killed Duhaut and Liotot, shocking the watching Indians with this display of treachery toward his friends.

For a while after this incident, the party stayed together, but at last Joutel and the Abbe Jean and five others gathered the courage to request that they be allowed to go to Canada; and surprisingly Hiens granted their request, demanding only that they sign a statement absolving him of any blame in the death of La Salle. This they did, after which he furnished them with supplies and they departed.

Joutel and the others journeyed for about two months through the wilderness, during which time De Marle was lost when he drowned while bathing. Otherwise, they suffered no major mishaps; and finally, one day, approaching the Arkansas River, at a point not far above its junction with the Mississippi, they came across a wooden cross and near it a small house. Here to their joy they were greeted by fellow Frenchmen.

Henri de Tonty, La Salle's lieutenant in Canada, on learning that La Salle had landed on the Gulf, had decide to go to the relief of the colony and to make up a war party to cross the Rio Grande and add a new province to France. He had left Fort St. Louis in February, 1686, in a wooden canoe, with twenty-five Frenchmen and eleven Indians. During Holy Week he reached the mouth of the Mississippi, where La Salle was to have founded his colony. But La Salle was then floundering on the prairies of Texas, and Tonty, though he sent search parties east and west, found no trace of his leader. Finally he abandoned hope of finding him, and turned to retrace his steps to Canada. At a village of the Arkansas Indians he left six volunteer Frenchmen to keep watch for travelers from the Gulf. These were the men who now greeted Joutel and Abbe Jean.

While these events were taking place, the little fort on the Gulf was nearing the end of its strength. La Salle had left in the fort about twenty people, among them seven women. To sustain them while awaiting La Salle's return, they had seventy or seventy-five swine, some chickens and meal, with whatever they could take from the country around them. They had still their eight pieces of cannon, and some powder and lead.

Their greatest fears were of the surrounding Indians, of discovery by the Spanish, and of famine. But the first tragedy that struck them was none of these; instead they were prostrated by an epidemic of smallpox, which took many of their lives. Weakened by this, they were unable to maintain a defense when they were attacked by Indians in 1689. Almost all of them were killed and a few children were taken captive in the attack, and much of the fort was destroyed.

In spite of La Salle's efforts to keep the purpose of his expedition from France a secret, the Spanish undoubtedly knew of the existence of the colony. If the crew of the captured *St. Francis* did not reveal the information, deserters from La Salle's company at Petit Goave probably did. And in 1684 a French corsair was captured off the coast of Yucatan, and "its crew confirmed the intelligence that La Salle sought to plant his colony at the mouth of the Mississippi. Consequently, Spanish expeditions cruised the waters of the Gulf and skirted the coast line incessantly searching for the intruders. . . ."

In 1687 the Spanish had found the wrecks of the *Belle* and the *Amiable*, from which they took four pieces of artillery and three painted fleurs-de-lis as evidence that the expedition had perished. Even after this, however, five expeditions were sent out by sea and four by land in search of survivors. In 1689 one of these, led by Alonzo de Leon, discovered the remains of the fort, and a priest accompanying him, Father Massenet, claimed that he personally set fire to the fort, destroying what was left of it.

So ended the hopes of France to found a new empire on the Gulf and seize the Spanish mines in Mexico, and so too ended the dreams of one of the greatest explorers of the American continent. Not for another hundred and fifty years would the French attempt to establish themselves in the land that would be Texas. Fort St. Louis on Lavaca Bay, though it was not what had been planned, was not a total failure. It established a French claim to Texas soil, and it stimulated Spain to occupy the Texas area and establish missions there. Later Frenchmen, too, would have a more direct influence on the course of Texas history than did its founder; but La Salle's intrepid spirit and faith in the new land are a memorable part of the legacy of the French in Texas. Monuments in Calhoun, Grimes, and Matagorda counties memorialize La Salle and Fort St. Louis and the part they played in fixing the eyes of Europe on Texas shores.

The Spanish

1519 - 1821

The Capture of the Nolan Expedition -- March 4, 1801

Philip Nolan

By
JAMES M. DAY

He lived just about thirty years, a relatively short time for a man. His death was a brave one, but inglorious and seemingly unnecessary. His friends bore stained reputations and his own motives were usually suspect. He was much of a gambler who had much to gain and much to lose; he played a daring hand using his life as the stakes. By his own deal, Philip Nolan chose to die in battle rather than be captured by the Spanish soldiers he had come to distrust. Such a short life-span seemingly should not produce the far-reaching results that came from Nolan's daring escapades on the prairies of Texas.

Nolan himself was not so dangerous to the Spaniards as was the type of person he represented. Spain had been in Texas since 1519, and even though her empire was crumbling, she managed to acquire the Louisiana Territory at the Peace of Paris in 1763. Prior to that date, Texas had been needed as a buffer zone against French encroachment on Mexico, but afterwards, with the removal of the French threat, the Spanish policy shifted. The period from 1763 to 1821, the year the Mexican Republic weaned itself, is generally conceded to be a time of readjustment in Texas; the transfer of Louisiana to France in 1800 and its purchase in 1803 by the United States aided and abetted the suspicion.

This shift was necessary because of the growing threat of conquest from intruders. Louisiana harbored many Spanish vassals who were to be distrusted along with the Frenchmen, while England was openly antagonistic owing to her commercial interest in the Spanish colonies. Most to be feared were the aggressive, land-hungry Anglo-Americans who pressed for the soil much as a termite does for wood. Spanish officials regarded these Americans with a jaundiced eye, and Philip Nolan was precisely the type that awed them. Two other concerns complicated the situation. First, the Spaniards had to deal with and placate the Texas Indians, some of whom were the most ferocious savages in the world. Then, as an added deterrent, Spain had imposed such an unwieldy administrative system on the region that real accomplishment in reform was impossible, and speedy legal proceedings were unknown. Quick justice was hard to come by.

At the head of Spain's administrative policy was the king, a divine right monarch. In this case, the ruler was King Charles IV, who reigned from 1788 to 1808. Two appointive councils, the Council of the Indies and the House of Trade, assisted him, especially the Council of the Indies which served as the highest court of appeal and was the legislative body for colonial affairs. An appointive viceroy in Mexico City was the king's counterpart, and under him a governor in each province acted as both military and political commander. In addition to his financial responsibilities, the governor confirmed municipal elections, issued licenses, served as the highest judge in the province, and commanded the military force assigned to his area. Interspersed between the viceroy and the governor of Texas was the commandant general of the Interior Provinces. The viceroys of Mexico during Nolan's time were Juan Vicente Revillagigedo, Second Marqués of Revillagigedo (1789-1794), Miguel de la Grua Talamante y Branciforte, the Marqués de Branciforte (1794-1798), Miguel José de Azanza (1798-1800), and Felix Berenguer de Marquina (1800-1803). Pedro de Nava held the post of commandant general of the Interior Provinces, consisting of Nuevo Vizcaya, Sonora, Sinaloa, California, New Mexico, Texas Coahuila, Nuevo León, and Nuevo Santander. His tenure extended from 1790 to 1802, so he watched Nolan arrive on the Texas scene, expand operations, and bring about his own destruction. The governors of Texas with whom Nolan worked were Manuel Muñoz (1790-1799) and Juan Bautista Elguezabal (1799-1805).

Louisiana, incorporated into the Spanish empire in 1783, was under the control of the captain-general of Cuba, and as such was entirely separated from New Spain, the Interior Provinces, and Texas. Resulting from this administrative break were such benefits as lower taxes, consequently goods could be taken into Texas and Mexico cheaper through Louisiana than other ports of entry. Spanish regulations strictly prohibited this trade, but nonetheless smugglers operated in abundance and especially so when they could persuade the Spanish officials to wink an eye at what they were doing. Nolan used this situation effectively to become a master of deceitful operations and to ingratiate himself with Spanish officials. The governors of Louisiana he met were Don Estevan Miro (1785-1791), Hector, Baron de Carondelet (1791-1797), Manuel Gayoso de Lemos (1797-1799), and Marqués de Caso Calvo (1799-1801). Carondelet was his good friend and protector, but the latter two were his implacable enemies. Still, Nolan was able to walk the tight-wire between life and death for about ten years before his passport from one province to the other proved to be his passport to death.

Nolan was born in Belfast, Ireland, in 1771. Just when he came to America cannot be determined; at first he lived in Maryland, but by 1788 he was living in the home of General James Wilkinson in Kentucky. In 1789 Nolan became Wilkinson's bookkeeper and shipping clerk in the general's tobacco concern. Nolan was such a strong lad that he could with one arm hoist a saddlebag containing two thousand pesos. After 1791 the youth was a free agent, but the bonds of friendship between the two never broke nor even weakened. Writing to Gayoso in 1790, Wilkinson noted that Nolan had lived as a member of his family for two years and that he had found Nolan to be "honorable, discreet, courageous, and active." Nolan was recommended to Gayoso "in the warmest manner." Wilkinson also claimed that Nolan was "a child of my own raising." The praise was not at all one-sided for Nolan could write to Wilkinson in 1791 "*I am wholly* yours until I do the business of the season." Another time Nolan mentioned that he could never forget "the friend and protector of my youth." This close friendship perhaps ultimately had a bearing on Nolan's death since Wilkinson was so closely connected with the Aaron Burr Conspiracy. The assumption has been made that Nolan was naturally involved as an agent. Spanish officials especially were suspicious of Nolan, while historians have usually been free in their accusations. Wilkinson, shrewd and duplicitious as he was, carefully destroyed most of his correspondence, so proof is lacking. Students, then, have been left to grasp at straws. Nolan could easily have worked for the United States' conquest of Spain's provinces, but the evidence available does not prove it.

His connection with Texas began in 1790 when Governor Miro of Louisiana issued him a passport to the Lone Star land for the purpose of gathering wild horses. Miro was able to grant the permission because of a royal decree dated 1780 which, recognizing the shortage of horses in Louisiana and their plentifulness in Texas, permitted Louisiana residents to enter Texas for this specific purpose. Nolan was perhaps the first Anglo-American to take advantage of this order; he became a mustanger. Since mustangs could sometimes be acquired by trading either with Indians or Texans, Nolan followed custom by carrying along a stock of merchandise. As time passed, Nolan could corral horses with the best of them but trading was easier, and Philip Nolan usually took the course leading to the best and quickest results. An English scientist named Francis Baily traveled with Nolan in 1797 and was impressed with Nolan's way of life. Baily wrote:

> He told me it was a life of extreme fatigue, and very difficult to be procured, as the Spanish governors were very jealous whom they admitted to this privilege; and it would be impossible to carry it on without their permission. His mode of carrying such articles as he takes out is in little barrels, which are placed upon packhorses, three

barrels upon a horse; and in this manner he will travel for hundd-dreds—I may say thousands, of miles through the woods, bartering with the Indians, as he goes along, and receiving in return skins and furs, or wild horses. These horses (of which there are plenty in the Apelousa country, and in the province of Mexico) are caught in a most curious manner, and which can only be effected with success by those who have been used to the practice.

Nolan was still in New Orleans in April, 1791, and apparently was still working for Wilkinson. A letter to Wilkinson dated April 6 shows that he had access to Governor Miro and that is probably how he gained his passport. Sometime later in that year he was in Nacogdoches on his first big mustanging venture. His optimistic hopes were soon turned into despairing thought because Miro was not able to protect him. Texas authorities, ever suspicious, took him to be a spy and threatened to imprison him. Nolan escaped this fate even though the goods were quickly taken from him, leaving him "reduced as poor as any Indian who tramps the forest."

Then, tired of civilization and its cares, he left the Spaniards to wander among the Indians. He thought that "the freedom, the independence of the savage life" would be pleasing to his nature, so he roamed among the Comanches and the Tawayes between the Illinois and San Antonio Rivers. For two years he lived like an Indian, becoming successful at hunting and victorious in "little feats of activity." Yet he found that he could not "Indianfy" his heart; he remembered that he had been the "only hope of a fond parent," that his trading venture had made him a debtor, so he returned to Spanish civilization determined to make another effort at commerce. Bringing fifty head of mustangs with him, Nolan went to New Orleans in 1794 where Governor Carondelet believed him to be "a person risen from the dead." One can surmise that he learned much of the woods, of wild horses, of Indians, and of Spaniards on this trip. Its import cannot be minimized.

Almost immediately Nolan set out for San Antonio on what he called his second trip to Texas. With him were five Louisiana citizens and a Negro slave, and he carried a passport from Carondelet. By June 6, 1794, he was in Nacogdoches where Christopher Córdoba, the Spanish commandant, honoring the Carondelet document, gave Nolan permission to do his mustanging. After several months he went on to San Antonio, arriving on December 21. There he talked with Texas Governor Manuel Muñoz about the possibility of legally introducing trade goods to be used in bartering for horses. Muñoz was favorably disposed so the matter was referred to Pedro de Nava, Muñoz's superior. Nava stated that Nolan could make a petition directly to him and he would approve the plan. Nolan seems to have been feeling out Muñoz rather than seeking actual permission, for the evidence, or lack of it, indicates that the matter was not pursued. Instead, a series of letters passed between Muñoz and Carondelet as both governors tacitly implied their approval of the trade Nolan proposed. Muñoz issued orders to Córdoba at Nacogdoches to guide Nolan with proper instructions, but to keep the matter strictly confidential, to discuss it with only one other person, José María Guadiana, and Nolan. Particularly, the people of Nacogdoches were not to know that Nolan was to have an opportunity to engage in this forbidden trade. Seemingly, the Irishman was well on his way to making a profitable venture.

Bringing with him 250 head of horses, Nolan was in Natchez by the end of 1795, where he left the horses before going to New Orleans to pay his respects to Carondelet. On June 9, 1796, he arrived at Frankfort, Kentucky. He had lost some of his animals from a sickness he called "yellow water" and distemper, had sold some at Natchez, and carried forty-two of them on to Frankfort. There he addressed a communication to his friend Wilkinson, explaining that he had not written sooner because a "letter from a trader in horses, to a General in the federal armies would have confirmed suspicions that were almost fatal." Already, the Spaniards were "ungenerously" suspecting him of being a spy. Then Nolan summarized his activities briefly and expressed regret that he had no horse worthy of Wilkinson's saddle. He had selected one that was "white as snow" and "all obedience," but it had been the first one to die of the distemper. Nevertheless, he promised the general a five-year-old bay which he, Nolan, would deliver personally in a short while. He made a further commitment that next spring he would deliver to Wilkinson a charger "fit for a warrior."

Just as Nolan saw the promise of success, a new wrinkle appeared. The Treaty of San Lorenzo (sometimes called Pinckney's Treaty) was signed in 1795 between Spain and the United States. The treaty had to do with navigation rights on the Mississippi River, an item extremely important to the western merchants, and it set about defining the boundaries between the two countries. Natchez and all territory east of the Mississippi and north of the two Floridas was surrendered to the United States. The part that concerned Nolan was the section which called for boundary commissioners to establish definite regions of control. Andrew Ellicott was appointed by the United States and Manuel Gayoso de Lemos served for Spain. While both Carondelet and Gayoso stalled because they did not want to relinquish the land, Ellicott arrived in Natchez in February, 1797, to begin work. Both of the commissioners were important to Nolan: one, Gayoso, became his determined enemy, while the other, Ellicott, eventually led him to be recognized and queried by Thomas Jefferson on matters of interest concerning Louisiana.

Nolan had a chance meeting with Ellicott in January, 1797, at the mouth of the Ohio River. Some have speculated that the meeting was not accidental but rather that Nolan sought out Ellicott in order to give him a proper view on the actions of James Wilkinson. Ellicott had already been warned by President George Washington to be watchful of Wilkinson, who had been mentioned as one "improperly connecting" himself with the Spanish government. Nolan naturally wanted to counter such an attitude; perhaps that is why he met Ellicott before the commissioner arrived at Natchez. He explained that Wilkinson's involvement with the Spaniards was purely commercial, but that the general had to pursue "a deceptive policy" and maintain "fictitious appearances" in order to protect Nolan's Texas-Louisiana trading activities.

The two men talked, became amicable, and went on to Natchez together. As they conversed, Nolan answered questions asked by the curious Ellicott, and in so doing provided the commissioner with facts he later found to be "extremely useful." Once, when Ellicott showed surprise at the Spaniards' delaying tactics in regard to the treaty, Nolan gave him some advice. He told the commissioner to suppress his suspicions; that he, Nolan, would provide Ellicott with such information as could be discovered; that such a policy of cooperation was essential "both for your success and my own safety." With this one diplomatic maneuver, Nolan explained Wilkinson's position to Ellicott and himself joined a conspiracy with the commissioner against the Spaniards. The only items involved here were Ellicott's mission (he did want to be successful) and Nolan's life. Such stakes provided an interesting game.

Nolan left Natchez and went on to New Orleans to secure a passport to Texas from Carondelet; likewise, he had to placate Gayoso. Carondelet proved an easy mark for the mustanger as Nolan explained that a small quarrel had grown up between Ellicott and Gayoso, and he, Nolan, had had to stay with the American commissioner for two nights to help tranquilize him. Then Carondelet is reported to have stated his intention of settling the Natchez trouble once and for all by giving the inhabitants "hemp" and the Americans "lead." Carondelet asked Nolan if he would take "an active part," and Nolan replied "a very active one." It seems that Nolan had learned much about duplicity from his mentor, Wilkinson; however, he had been among the Spaniards, some of whom were also adept at intrigue. Without difficulty Nolan obtained his passport from Carondelet.

Gayoso was not so gullible as Carondelet, nor did he trust Nolan, but the mustanger knew that Gayoso was scheduled to replace Carondelet when the governorship of Louisiana changed. Gayoso definitely was important to Nolan. Negotiations between the two started March 13, 1797, when Gayoso specifically asked Nolan what "political interest" he embraced. Nolan wrote on the same sheet of paper "Spain—& properly encouraged would take an active part—not as a negociator, but a warrior." Gayoso was not satisfied so he asked definition of the terms "negociator" and "warrior." This time Nolan gave a more considered reply, explaining that he "would do what is honorable and detest everything mean." He stated his intention of telling Ellicott that he, Nolan, was a Spaniard, and that "the part I have already acted was with a view to promote the interest of both countries." Since the rumor was spreading that the British soon planned an invasion of Spanish territory, Nolan stated his willingness to serve Spain "on the Missouri" or in "any other enterprise that may be honourable." All of this correspondence passed between the two men on the same day.

Upon reflection, Nolan was not satisfied that Gayoso had been convinced. The next day he decided to offer the Spaniard half of the profits from the proposed commercial venture Nolan had been so deliberately proposing. After acquainting Gayoso with the basic facts of the situation, Nolan delivered his broadside blast when he wrote:

> Properly recommended by yr. Excellency and the Baron I have not a doubt but I can make an arrangement with him that at *one stroke* will make our fortunes. I can command merchandise. — I will require nothing but your Excellency's protection council and advise and will consider you entitled to half the profits. —If this plan should meet your excellency's approbation I would set out immediately and return in time to perform the voyage next winter.

The ruse worked. Gayoso, flattered by the offer, used two weeks to think it over before he accepted. On April 1, 1797, he took opportunity to praise profusely Nolan's "energy, knowledge, good reputation and . . . genius for comprehension." Gayoso had waited a long time for the opportunity to express the "sincere affection" he felt for Nolan, but because the trader had "not had time to acquire experience," his character had had to be tested. Gayoso concluded: "No one better knows your worth; also no one more than I, interests himself more in the advancement of your fortunes."

From the Treaty of San Lorenzo, then, Nolan seized the opportunity to make friends with Ellicott, gain the confidence of Gayoso, and obtain his passport from Carondelet. By April 24, 1797, Nolan could communicate to Wilkinson to report success. He wrote:

> I have got such a passport, that I apprehend neither risk nor detention; I have instruments to enable me to make a more correct map than the one you saw; Ellicott assisted me in acquiring a more perfect knowledge of astronomy and glasses; and Gayoso himself has made me a present of a portable sextant. My time piece is good. I shall pay every attention, and take an assistant with me who is a tolerable mathematician.

Carondelet actually issued the passport on June 17, 1797, recommending Nolan to the Texas governor Muñoz. He provided for Nolan, William Escot, John Murdock, two Negroes and four Spaniards to procure horses for Louisiana, and at the same time instructed his own commandants not to interfere and begged "those outside his jurisdiction" to do likewise. In a letter to Muñoz the next day, Carondelet stated Nolan's purpose of acquiring horses, noting that "This young man will not deviate from a strict obedience to our laws, nor from any particular order that you may give him." With Carondelet, his known successor Gayoso, and Muñoz the Texas governor in one accord as to the enterprise, Nolan could at that time see no possibility of Spanish hindrance.

Yet such was soon to come. The controversy at Natchez grew to larger proportions; the people of Natchez humiliated Gayoso and drove him from the town; and the American general named Wilkinson secured the place for the United States. Gayoso then warned Carondelet to seize Wilkinson's agent, Nolan, but the Baron refused to do so. What a difference one month can bring! Nolan, aware that Gayoso was trying to stop his activities, wrote to Wilkinson on July 21 that: "I may yet be obliged to shoot the monster, with a poisoned arrow." His life would have been safer if he had, for Gayoso never did release the pressure once he had begun to apply it. Gayoso called for Nolan's arrest on the one hand and treated him "with attention" on the other, but Nolan knew him as "a vile man, and my implacable enemy." If Nolan became a master of deceit, it is no wonder because he had Wilkinson and Gayoso as examples and teachers. Both were excellent models.

Nevertheless, Nolan continued preparations for the venture. He collected $7,000 worth of merchandise and commanded twelve good rifles, although one of them would, as Nolan thought, be manned by a coward.

John Murdock of Natchez, taken in as a junior partner, was to provide $2,400 worth of merchandise in return for one-third of the net profit and the instruction that Nolan would provide concerning mustanging. Nolan wanted the money; Murdock the experience. Seemingly, Nolan considered canceled his proposed partnership with Gayoso.

About the time Nolan set out for Texas in late July, 1797, Carondelet was succeeded by Gayoso as governor of Louisiana and Nolan's real trouble began. Gayoso wrote Viceroy Branciforte advising that all foreigners entering Texas be arrested, because some of them were wanting to make friends with the Indians and use that friendship to start a revolution. Nolan especially was to be considered dangerous. By February 12, 1798, Branciforte had communicated this information to Pedro de Nava, commandant general of the Interior Provinces, who was by then wondering what should be done about Nolan and his proposals. Gayoso had done his work.

Nolan in the meantime had gone to Nacogdoches, where he acted as interpreter in an investigation concerning Lucas Ose, and on to San Antonio where he counseled with Muñoz. Nolan at that time proposed that he be allowed to go to Nuevo Santander for the horses he needed. He claimed that Carondelet had authorized this, but he could not produce the letter. Carondelet, queried at his South American post, denied issuing Nolan any such authority. After a round of correspondence between Muñoz, Branciforte, Nava, Carondelet, and the Count of Sierra Gorda (governor of Nuevo Santander), Nolan finally was denied his request. Nava had almost been persuaded to grant it, but instructions arrived from Branciforte to the contrary, so Nava issued the denying order to Muñoz. Administratively, Nolan was prohibited from going to Nuevo Santander and further was stopped from introducing 2,000 pesos worth of trade goods into Texas. All foreigners in Texas were to be arrested, but Nolan, since he already had a legal passport, could stay on to collect his horses. Yet, even to accomplish this much, Nava had to assure Branciforte that Nolan would be immediately deported if anything he did appeared to oppose the king.

Such was the state of affairs when José Miguel de Azanza became viceroy about the middle of the year 1798. With him came another round of inquiries about Nolan. Azanza quizzed Carondelet about Nolan's passport and received the same legalistic replies about the Decree of 1780; he quizzed Nava and received mostly favorable reports on Nolan. Then, in September, Azanza finally advised Nava to use the utmost tact in ordering Nolan to leave Texas. Nava had a letter from Nolan in which the mustanger stated that his departure time was near; consequently

Nava told Azanza that the matter was settled. Nava indicated that Nolan had already left Texas and that none of his movements showed he had acted detrimentally to the Spanish interest. The viceroy was satisfied.

Nava, though, was in for a surprise. Seven months later, on April 30, 1799, Muñoz informed him that several Comanches had had to be punished for stealing Nolan's horses. Nava immediately issued a reply that he thought Nolan had left Texas a year before; that Nolan must now leave Texas quickly; and that he must never be allowed to return to the province. Nava's suspicions were aroused by Nolan's extended stay so he asked for Muñoz's frank opinion about the mustanger. It was not long in coming. Muñoz explained that he had watched Nolan from the day he arrived in Texas, and that the horse trader had done nothing to arouse suspicion. He believed that Nolan's lengthy visit was caused by the many obstacles that had to be overcome: the building of corrals and pastures on the Trinity River and the taking of the horses there in small herds. Besides, Nolan's trip to Nuevo Santander had taken much time. Even though Nolan had been forbidden to go there, he had done so anyway, and neither Nava nor the viceroy had been informed of it. Muñoz was convinced that Nolan was loyal to Spain and that should the Americans invade Spanish territory, Nolan could be depended on to rush to the Spanish cause. Muñoz felt sure he could control Nolan because the two were good friends.

In reply to Nava's order that Nolan leave Texas immediately, Muñoz explained that Nolan had gained permission to go back to Louisiana on April 27, only three days before the receipt of the order. He went on to explain that the American had acquired 1,206 head of horses, enough to fulfill his contract, and that he might still be on the Trinity conditioning the animals for the trip eastward. Muñoz stated that a lieutenant would be sent to tell Nolan that he, like all other foreigners, was excluded from Texas. No such party was dispatched, so Nolan never knew the full extent of his danger. Muñoz died on July 27, 1799, so he was not punished for his previous dilatory conduct.

By November 12, 1799, Nolan and his horses were at Natchez, in the jurisdiction of the United States. His two years in Texas had been active ones. While Spanish officials were concerned with what he could and could not do, Nolan was actually doing just as he pleased. On the Trinity River he built his corrals; at San Antonio he established a household; and he collected his horses and mules along the Rio Grande. John Murdock, his partner, stayed in Texas for a while, but he either tired of the life, or felt he had had enough experience with mustanding, or was needed in Louisiana to gather trading material. Murdock returned to Natchez while Nolan continued to make arrangements for the venture's success. Nolan hired a personal servant, Peter Guervas Longueville, and a helper, Jesse Cook, whom he paid twelve dollars per month. Two of his important aides were Anthony Leal and his wife Gertrudis de los Santos (usually called St. Gertrude). The Leals had met Nolan in Nacogdoches in 1791 and a friendship had developed. In 1795 Leal was invited to stay at Nolan's house in San Antonio, but Leal and St. Gertrude lived with someone else. When Nolan returned to San Antonio in 1797, the Leals moved in with him and established a common household. The Leals had land in East Texas where the town of San Augustine is now located and Nolan's Trinity pasture was nearby. In addition to trading for his own interest on occasion, Leal was also sent to Louisiana with horses from Nolan. He was kept busy traveling. Often he carried "dressed deer skins, venison, tallow, tongues" to New Orleans, and once he delivered 115 horses of Nolan's to Natchez.

While he was away, his wife St. Gertrude was performing other services for "Don Felipe Nolan." She was about forty years of age when the two met in 1791 and an enterprising woman. After the common housekeeping arrangement of 1797, Nolan promised to build a house for her, and she engaged in horse trading in her own name. Moreover, by her own admission, she was a "frail woman" who engaged in "illicit intercourse" with Nolan. Her price was $4,000 and two hundred horses, which Nolan promised to pay. Longueville thought their "evil friendship" was "notorious," and he was able to recall a trip the two took together to Laredo and Revilla (now Guerrero) in the province of Nuevo Santander. They returned to San Antonio with 150 tame horses and mules. Their relationship proved itself on August 20, 1798, when St. Gertrude, at age 47, presented Nolan with a "natural daughter" named María Josefa. She was baptized at San Fernando church nine days later with Juan José and Josefa Leal as godparents, and she was listed in the church register as Nolan's daughter.

As Nolan's third expedition climaxed, Anthony Leal went with him to Natchez and St. Gertrude moved on to Nacogdoches. Early in 1800, Leal returned to Nacogdoches where he and his wife were arrested. Taken to San Antonio along with Jesse Cook and Peter Longueville, they were queried as to their part in Nolan's supposed conspiracy. Eventually, they were freed, and Anthony Leal died in 1802. St. Gertrude then married Antonio Baca, commandant at Bexar, whom she also outlived.

Another accomplishment of Nolan's third expedition had to do with his scientific discoveries. His contact at New Orleans was Daniel Clark,

Jr., a fellow Irishman and a successful merchant. Clark had worked in the office of the Spanish governor of Louisiana and then for a while in 1798 was temporary American Consul at New Orleans. Later Jefferson appointed him regular consul at New Orleans, he was actively involved in the Burr Conspiracy, and he served a term in the United States Congress. To this man Nolan entrusted the right to "peruse all Letters." He did this to prevent awakening "the jealousy of the suspicious people among whom he has by a coincidence of fortunate circumstances introduced himself."

One letter which came into Clark's hands was from Thomas Jefferson, then vice-president. It was written in Philadelphia on June 24, 1798. Jefferson, who was curious about all things and especially the West, had heard of Nolan's activities from one of the Kentucky senators. He wanted to know about the "large herds of wild horses in the country West of the Mississippi." The information, Jefferson thought, would add an interesting chapter to the studies of the Americal Philosophical Society; Nolan was the "sole reliance" for "obtaining this desideratum." If, by chance, Nolan did not have opportunity to impart all of his knowledge in one letter, later communications would be "thankfully received."

Almost eight months later the letter was in Clark's hands. He replied favorably to Jefferson as follows:

> You judge right in supposing him to be the only person capable of fulfilling your Views as no person of his talents has ever visited that Country to unite information with projects of utility. Shortly after his return, but not before on acct. of the impossibility of applying himself during his travels with that attention he could wish to the subject, I will be responsible for his giving you every information he has collected, and it will require all the good Opinion you may have been led to entertain of his veracity not to have your Belief staggered with the accounts you will receive of the numbers. & habits of the horses of that Country and the people who live in that Neighborhood whose Customs & ideas are as different from ours as those of the Hordes of Grand Tartary.

Clark was as enthusiastic to serve Jefferson as he was to serve Nolan, but he suggested that all future correspondence be addressed to him, Clark, at New Orleans to prevent the "most fatal consequences" to Nolan. He thought that Nolan had it in his power to "render important Services to the U. S." because "Nature seems to have formed [him] for Enterprizes of which the rest of Mankind are incapable." "Should any accident happen which would deprive the World of this extraordinary Character," Clark and another friend had possession of his papers, and they would forward to Jefferson any information contained therein. Finally, Clark mentioned that William Dunbar of Natchez was also knowledgeable of scientific subjects.

Clark was at Natchez with Dunbar in 1799 when Nolan returned from the wilderness. On November 12, Clark addressed another letter to Jefferson explaining the circumstances of Nolan's escape from Texas. Clark made the movements appear like a cloak and dagger melodrama with Nolan as the hero and the Spanish officials, especially Gayoso, as the villains. He overdrew the plot perhaps, but "Nolan might probably have been confined for life on mere suspicion." Certainly, had the Spaniards known that a person of Jefferson's high station was corresponding with Nolan, the man would not have been allowed to live. Clark concluded that Nolan "proposes shortly forwarding you the information you require."

Wilkinson was the one to finally introduce Nolan to Jefferson. His letter, dated May 22, 1800, read as follows:

> In the Bearer of this Letter—Mr. P. Nolan, you will behold the Mexican traveller, a specimen of whose discoveries, I had the Honor to submit to you in the Winter 1797, M. N—s subsequent excursions have been more extensive, & his observations more accurate, He feels pride in offering Himself to your investion, and I am persuaded you will find pleasure, in his details of a Country, the Soil, clime, population, movements & productions of which are so little known to us.

Evidence is lacking as to whether Jefferson and Nolan ever actually met, but it is interesting to speculate that the vice-president of the United States shared a pleasant visit with the mustanger from Texas—a man who had ingratiated himself into the Spanish official system of Mexico from the viceroy to the commandant of Nacogdoches, thereby causing them several moments of anxious agony.

Perhaps Jefferson's interest led later students to the conclusion that Nolan had produced a small book on Texas. In 1887 one of Texas' foremost geologists, Robert T. Hill, announced in his pamphlet, *The Present Condition of the Knowledge of the Geology of Texas*, (U. S. Geological Survey *Bulletin* No. 45) that Nolan had "published a small work accompanied by a topographic map" after his arrival in Natchez in 1799. Hill thought this was the first description of Texas written by an actual observer that had been printed in the United States, but he negated its importance by stating that "The results were trifling, the map was incorrect and restricted, and moreover, the book is practically out of existence."

Unfortunately, Hill did not cite his source. Then in 1896 C. W. Raines in his *Bibliography of Texas* picked up the Hill notation and supplied the following: "Nolan, Philip. Description of Texas; with topographic man. 18 mo. Natchez, Miss., 1799. Map faulty, and book out of print and perhaps out of existence." There the matter stood until Douglas C. McMurtrie dispelled the legend in his *Preliminary Check List of Mississippi Imprints,* 1798-1810 (Chicago, 1934). After correspondence between V. Valta Parma, curator of the Rare Book Room of the Library of Congress and Robert T. Hill, Parma concluded that Hill had picked up his entry from a conference with Edward Everett Hale. Hale thought he had seen the map in the Library of Congress, but it was never found. McMurtrie concluded: "The facts as now known do not appear to justify inclusion of the Nolan title in a bibliography of early Mississippi imprints."

The fact is that Nolan did not make a map of Texas. Jesse Cook explained how Nolan, on his second expedition, had made an abstract which he "formed" into a map and presented to the Baron de Carondelet. Nolan, in a letter to Wilkinson dated June 10, 1796, made mention of the fact that Wilkinson had seen this map. Moreover, with the instruments carried on the third expedition, Nolan had hopes of making a better one, but the proof that he did is inconclusive. Still, having planned to do so, one can speculate that he did. Perhaps he showed it to Jefferson; perhaps not.

For about a year Nolan remained along the banks of the Mississippi. His associations—Wilkinson, Clark, Dunbar and others—afforded him acceptance into a society which no doubt was eager to hear of his daring exploits and narrow escapes. As he socialized he met the girl he later married. She was Frances Lintot, daughter of William Lintot, a wealthy planter who was also the father-in-law of Stephen Minor, one-time Spanish commandant at Natchez. The wedding took place at Natchez on December 19, 1799, but Nolan lived with her less than a year before he left for Texas on his fourth and final expedition. She bore him a son, a namesake, six months after he left; then she died shortly afterwards. Philip Nolan, Jr. lived only twenty-one years before he too expired. He never saw his father.

During the summer of 1800 Nolan began to prepare for a new sortie to Texas. He said he had some horses there and needed to get them. After his application for a passport had been refused by the new Louisiana governor, Caso Calvo, Nolan proceeded with his plans anyway. As he set about to enlist recruits, the Spanish consul for the Natchez area, José Vidal, became suspicious. He reported the activities to Caso Calvo and the Spaniards became apprehensive. Vidal thought Nolan had enough men to defend against any force. Nolan, openly defiant of Spanish authority, offered men pay in horses, the average being five horses per man for three months work. Each man was to provide his own working horses and arms, help in the building of corrals, and assist in catching the mustangs. Nolan was to furnish the food and ammunition, and pay a *peso* per day to each man if the trip lasted longer than three months.

The more Nolan recruited, the more Vidal became interested in the project. The more Vidal learned, the more he became determined to put a halt to it. In a letter to Caso Calvo on September 27, 1800, Vidal noted that Nolan had boasted that he could whip one hundred Spaniards with twenty men. Nolan's "perfect knowledge of all the strategic places" was "superior to that of the natives," and he was "capable, enterprising, and shrewd." His acquaintance with the land was so thorough that he even intended to enter Texas by a new and unknown route, a mysterious one that would enable him to win several tribes of Indians to his cause. Vidal thought this cause was the overthrow of the Spanish government in Texas. Vidal further hurled a dart at the negligence of the United States government for allowing such an evil enterprise to be formed within its boundaries.

Vidal then registered a complaint against Nolan with Governor Winthrop Sargent of the Mississippi Territory. In asking Sargent to stop the activity, Vidal predicted its outcome by stating that an armed force would suppress the expedition and the consequences would be fatal. Sargent reacted by ordering Nolan to appear before the Supreme Court of the territory. Nolan, upon interrogation, admitted he was planning to cross the Mississippi to get some horses belonging to him, but that he did so with Pedro de Nava's permission. Nava, the commandant general of the Interior Provinces, wanted Nolan to map the routes connecting Louisiana with Texas and the Interior Provinces. His permission had been obtained in 1798, Nolan stated. In the face of such testimony, the court judges decided they could not issue a preventive order; that they could not act until a violation had been committed. Nolan was free to go.

And go he did after enlisting men, an easier job now than before the trial. Twenty-seven men were signed on, including eighteen Americans, seven Spaniards, and two Negroes.

Nolan's men, as listed by their captor, Miguel de Músquiz, were:

The Spaniards: Luciano García, 39, native of Real de Charcas, and resident of Nacogdoches; Vicente Lara, 38, native of the abandoned presidio of Orcoquisac, and citizen of Bexar; Refugio de la Garza, 25, native of Cadereyta; Juan Joseph Martínez, 30, native of Salinas, Nuevo León, and citizen of Nacogdoches; Lorenzo Inojosa,

31, native of the Villa of Camargo, Nuevo Santander, citizen of Bexar; Joseph Berban, 19, native of Nacogdoches; and Joseph the Jesús de los Santos, native of the Presidio of Bahía del Espíritu Santo.

The Americans: Simon McKoy, 23, native of Opelousas, Louisiana and a resident of Natchez for five years; Jonah Watters, 24, native of [the capital] of Virginia; Zalmon Cooley, 25, native of Queniteque [Kentucky], and resident of Natchez for two years; Ellis Bean, 22, native of North Carolina, and resident of Natchez on eyear; Joseph Reed, 26, native of the capital of Pennsylvania, and resident of Natchez a year and half; William Danlin, 17, native of Pennsylvania, and resident of Natchez eleven years; Charles King, 27, native of [Gerston?] Maryland, and resident of Natchez a year and a half; Stephen Richards, 19, native of Pennsylvania, and a resident of Natchez; [Joel] Joseph Pierce, 22, native of North Carolina, and a resident of Natchez a year and a half; Thomas House, 25, native of Virginia, and a resident of Natchez for a year and nine months; Ephraim Blackburn, 35, native of Notenjan [?], Maryland, and a resident of Natchez five years; David Fero, 24, native of New York, and a resident of Natchez for a year and half; Juan Bautista, negro, (known by the Americans, as Cesar), 46, native of the Island of Granada France; Robert Ashley, 38, native of South Carolina, resident of Natchez eight years; John House, 21, native of Virginia, and resident of Natchez one year; Michael Moore, 25, native of Ireland, resident of Natchez for six years; and the negro Robert, 24, native of Maryland and resident of Natchez two years.

In addition, three others who deserted before the group reached Texas were Mordecai Richards, John King, and August Adams.

The persistent Vidal hounded the group every step of the way. His warning tipped off the Spaniards at Rapides, Louisiana, concerning a letter that Nolan's slave, José de los Santos, was carrying to Jesse Cook at Nacogdoches. Santos was arrested and the letter confiscated. In it Nolan stated his plans to take an inland route to the Rio Grande, but since Vidal had discovered his intentions, he would go along the coast. The objective, as stated in the letter was Revilla (Guerrero) on the Rio Grande, where everything was so well arranged that he would not be detained for two days. He told Cook to gather up their horses and "drive them off," or they would all be lost. Intriguingly he wrote: "I take with me a large stock of goods, and they all think I am going to run mustangs." The sentence, written on October 23, 1800, whets the intellectual appetite and makes one want to know more of his real intentions, which perhaps were other than horses. Note, though, that his horses were not to be neglected.

At the very moment when Nolan was making his plans at Natchez, Pedro de Nava was preparing a Texas reception party for him. Belatedly, on August 8, 1800, he sent instructions to the new Texas governor, Juan Bautista Elguezábal, to arrest Nolan if he ever returned to Texas. Nava was convinced that Nolan had been in Texas for some reason other than "getting horses for the Louisiana regiment." Specifically, Elguezábal was to question Nolan on the following points: his location and movements for the last five or six years, his native country, his residence, his occupation, his religion, his American citizenship, whether he had commercial intercourse with citizens of the United States, whether he drove to that country horses and mules which he had bought in Texas and Louisiana from friendly Indians, and lastly, whether he had a commission from General Wilkinson. The Spaniards of Texas were ready for Nolan when he came.

Leaving Natchez on October 25, 1800, Nolan's men on horses thundered steadily toward their destiny. The leader of the force was confident that his superior knowledge of the terrain would prevent his detection, much less his arrest. Still, because of Vidal's persistent interruptions, Nolan changed his route a third time and presumably his plans to go to Revilla. Interestingly, the expedition did not carry the "large stock of goods" Nolan had intended to include; rather, all they took were provisions and such items as mustangers would need to catch, brand, and tame horses. Their trail took them up river to present Vicksburg, across the river and the land to the Ouachita River, near the Spanish post on the Ouachita, and on to Nacogdoches. The Spaniards had been alerted, and Vicente Fernández Tejiero, commandant at the Ouachita post, was prepared for Nolan. With nineteen Spanish soldiers, he met and faced Nolan's band. Nolan offered his passport but Tejiero demurred, stating that he was only hunting horse thieves. Since the Americans outnumbered the Spaniards almost two to one, Tejiero was polite and extremely discrete. He had been ready for Nolan, but not ready enough. Nolan was allowed to pass.

As he did so, Nolan dropped a note to Tejiero stating that he would not go near the garrisons commanded by Tejiero, that his objective was Texas. Brazenly Nolan informed the Spaniard that "I have not provided myself with a passport." As a result Tejiero the following day dispatched fifty Spanish soldiers to catch the invaders, but they could not do so. Nevertheless, Nolan's men became suspicious that he did not have the passport they had been told he had. Three of them deserted, fell into the hands of the Spaniards, and gave testimony against the American adventurer. Nolan spent about one week looking for the deserters before resuming his trip. He became cautious and took away the powder and ammunition to prevent others from leaving him.

Elguezábel at Bexar watched the movements and became convinced that Nolan was intending to form an alliance with the Indians in order to fall upon the settlements and rob and plunder with impunity. The governor sent agents among the Indians to observe any undue movements. Nolan's servant Peter Longueville, his agent Jesse Cook, and his friends Anthony and Gertrude Leal were arrested as they tried to drive their horses out of Spanish jurisdiction. Since Nolan had threatened to go to the Rio Grande, the governor of Nuevo Santander was alerted to the situation. He in turn sent troops scurrying over the countryside with orders to arrest all foreigners who did not hold a passport from the governor of Texas. The regular troops were busy patrolling, and the militia was called up and provided with food, arms, and horses. For four months the Spaniards guarded the Rio Grande looking for the elusive Nolan. Money and supplies became scarce, and men and mounts were tired. Spanish officials, from the viceroy to the local commandants, were concerned, but all they could do was watch and wait. They had some Indian scares and made a few inconsequential arrests, but Nolan never showed.

This evasion is easily explained. Nolan's band had passed north of Nacogdoches journeying to the lands on the Grand Prairie of Texas occupied by the Tawakoni Indians. There he set up camp, built a small fort, and proceeded to catch and tame his horses. He needed the fort as protection against the Indians, who resented his presence. Courageous as he was, he proceeded to do the work at hand.

The precise location of Nolan's camp has never been established and as a result most historians simply list it as being "near Waco." J. A. Quintero, writing in the *Texas Almanac* in 1868, stated that it was in present Limestone County near Springfield, or in McLennan County near Waco. David Donaghue of Fort Worth, writing in 1929, placed it near Blum in present Hill County.

Nolan placidly went about his business, kept his diary, and watched his force dwindle to twenty-five men. As the time lengthened beyond the three months he had intended to stay, more and more men deserted. As these events transpired, the Spaniards were not idle. They offered the Indians a reward of forty horses for delivery of Nolan, dead or alive. Also, the commandant at Nacogdoches, Miguel Músquiz, made it his business to locate the mustangers. With the assistance of William Barr, one of Nolan's fellow Irishmen, Músquiz located the group and organized a troop of one hundred men to eradicate the menace. Barr, a merchant at Nacogdoches, and Nolan had been enemies for about six years, so Barr went along for the slaughter. Interestingly enough, Nolan's boast that he could whip a hundred Spaniards with twenty men was about to be tested.

Músquiz, keeping a diary, left Nacogdoches on March 4, 1801. By the pre-dawn hours of the 21st his force had located Nolan's camp, had concealed themselves behind a hill, and were waiting for sunrise before attacking. Everything was in readiness; but a problem arose. With all of the movement, Nolan's horses became restless and he was thus alerted. Thinking that Indians were the cause he sent several men out to investigate. Only at daybreak did he realize the import of the restlessness.

Dividing themselves into three groups, each of which was larger than Nolan's force, the men of Músquiz advanced. Nolan, seeing the situation, turned to his men and urged them to fight till death because the Spaniards would make slaves of them. Then he rushed out to order the Spaniards to stop or "one of us will be killed." Músquiz halted to send Barr forward to order the surrender of the Americans. Barr and Nolan talked briefly, then separated, as Nolan returned to his fort to prepare for battle. Again, he urged his men to bravery; his Irish ire was up. Just at this point Nolan lost some of his men through capture and desertion, leaving his force at exactly twenty, his magic number.

Such was the status when the firing began, Músquiz using to advantage the small cannon he had brought along. About nine in the morning, Don Felipe Nolan was killed by a cannon ball. David Fero then assumed command as the mustangers fled to the woods, where they took refuge in a cave. Shortly, after a conference with a former companion, they surrendered, much to their later sorrow. The fighting was ended: Nolan had lost his boast and his life, and a dreaded menace had been removed from the Spanish frontier. To show proper hatred for Nolan and at the same time curry favor with his superiors, Músquiz cut off Nolan's ears and sent them to the governor at San Antonio. William Barr, an Irishman bearing Irish ears, took them personally to Elguezábal along with Músquiz's report and Nolan's personal papers. Only after the ears had been removed was the body allowed to be buried. Fittingly, it rests on the Texas prairies where Nolan's wild spirit had found kinship with the mustangs he loved to chase.

Philip Nolan, at age thirty, had played out his hand. He left behind a wife and a son and a lover and a daughter. His domain had spread from the Mississippi to the Rio Grande; it was a land he understood.

Duped though they were, Nolan's companions paid a high price for the association. They were taken to Nacogdoches and tried as invaders of Spanish land. About two hundred manuscript pages of testimony were taken and forwarded to San Antonio, but only after four of the men had escaped. In July the prisoners went to San Antonio, and then after three months they were taken to Saltillo as a legal problem arose as to whether the viceroy or the commandant general of the Interior Provinces had jurisdiction. From Saltillo the group went to San Luis Potosi and then to Chihuahua. Officials in Mexico were unable to decide on who should try them, so the king had to be consulted. Two years had passed since their capture before the trial began at Chihuahua, and another full year slipped by before the judge, Pedro Galindo Navarro, ordered them released. The new commandant general of the Interior Provinces, Nemesis Salcedo, objected to the order as some of the prisoners were moved from Chihuahua to the presidio of San Carlos. There they were allowed the privilege of living as they pleased within the town limits and even were permitted to adopt a trade.

An attempted escape plot failed so they were still in the depths of Mexico in 1806, when the American explorer Zebulon Montgomery Pike saw them and made an "ineffectual application" to "rescue them from the eternal slavery." Pike found it hard to believe that the court of Spain would not give liberty "to a few debilitated and half lost wretches, who have at least expiated their crime (if any) tenfold." Pike, who had some problems of confinement of his own when he saw Nolan's men, was visibly touched. Still relief for Nolan's survivors did not come. Their statements and accompanying documents were sent to Spain for another decision by the king. Finally, on February 23, 1807, almost six years after their capture, he rendered the verdict: one out of five would be hanged and the rest sentenced to ten years at hard labor at separate presidios. Only nine were left to cast dice for life or death, so the authorities agreed that only one should die. The fact that they were there proved their gambling blood, so the dice and cup were displayed as the game began. Ephraim Blackburn, a Quaker, was the oldest of the lot so he threw first. His 3 and 1 proved to be the low throw; accordingly on November 11, 1807, after he had been baptized as a Catholic, Blackburn was hanged in the Plaza de los Urangas in Chihuahua City. The others then began their ten years sentence.

Only two of Nolan's men were heard from again. David Fero, Ellis Peter Bean, and two others were sent to Acapulco. Fero and Bean were still there when the Mexican Revolution began in 1819. Fero was beheaded by the insurgent José María Morelos, but Bean survived and emerged as a colonel in the Mexican army. Later, after he returned to

Texas a saddened man, his memoirs were printed in Henderson Yoakum, *History of Texas* (2 vols.; New York, 1855-56), 403-452. Bean provided an interesting but biased narrative of Nolan's fourth and last expedition.

Nolan's activities were not so important in themselves as for what their threat represented to the Spaniards, who were tenuously holding a turbulent land. One would be hard pressed to label Nolan as a filibusterer, but he was later followed by a reckless breed of men who sought to atomize the Spanish empire for their own aggrandizement. James Long and Augustus Magee were only two of a long list of threatening Anglo-Americans who followed in Nolan's wake. Nolan, then, was the one who plowed the furrow that led straight to Spanish fear. As the fear expanded, it led to the Mexican revolution, and ultimately to the Texas revolution. As a result, Texas was lost both to Spain and Mexico and gained by the United States. Philip Nolan's mustanging activities had a part in making this possible.

The Mexican

1821 - 1836

The Death of Ben Milam -- December 7, 1835

The Siege and Storming of Bexar

By
Richard G. Santos

The short fifteen-year span of Mexican rule over Texas was a whirlwind of political and military unrest. Beginning with the overthrow of Spanish rule in 1821, Mexico underwent a political struggle between those who favored a republican system of government and those who favored a monarchy. The latter group won the first encounter, and Colonel Agustín de Iturbide was proclaimed emperor of the First Imperial Government of Mexico. Ten months later, however, he was overthrown and a provisional government installed. In January, 1824, the Republic of Mexico came into existence, and a new struggle developed between the federalists and centralists.

Under the Mexican Federal Constitution of 1824, Texas was annexed to Coahuila to form "The Free, Sovereign, and Independent State of *Coahuila y Tejas.*" The Department of Texas, ruled by a *Jefe Politico* entrusted to maintain order, enforce the laws and command the militia, was subject to the State Government at Saltillo, Coahuila. Like most of the States comprising the Republic of Mexico, Coahuila y Tejas was federalistic in nature and a strong supporter of States' rights.

Also in 1824, the Mexican National Congress adopted an immigration law honoring the previous and tentative *empressario* contracts by foreign settlers. The legislature of *Coahuila y Tejas* followed suit by passing a similar law in 1825. Families from the United States then flocked to Texas under the colonization contracts of Stephen F. Austin, Green De Witt, John McMullen, James McGloin and others.

Stephen Austin had a decisive advantage, however, of having fallen heir to the precursory work of his father, Moses Austin, who had received tentative approval to introduce settlers from the United States in December, 1820. The untimely death of Moses Austin left the unfinished task in the hands of his son Stephen. In August, 1821, Stephen Austin arrived at San Antonio to receive what he considered final approval for the enterprise, and his first settlers began to arrive in Texas four months later. The independence of Mexico from Spain and the ensuing political unrest, however, barred Austin from receiving official approval of his contract until 1824. Hereafter, Austin's colony was to become a model of foreign colonization in Texas.

Austin and the colonists, like the native *Coahuiltejanos*, were loyal Mexican federalists primarily concerned with their regional difficulties. Thus they were able to stay aloof from national politics until the passing of the National Emancipation Decree of 1829, which brought Coahuila y Texas into conflict with the National Government, as it would have abolished slavery in Texas. Ramón Músquiz, *Jefe Politico* at Bexar, withheld circulation of the decree and appealed to the Governor to exempt Texas from the law. The Governor of *Coahuila y Tejas* transmitted the appeal to the Mexican President who approved the request exempting the Department of Texas from the emancipation decree.

The next crisis occurred on April 6, 1830, when the Mexican National Congress passed a law which seemed to prohibit the further colonization of Texas by families from the United States. The decree also prohibited the further introduction of slaves into the Republic of Mexico. Although the contracts of Stephen Austin and Green De Witt were exempt from the stipulations of the decree, the damage had been done. This law thus became the turning point in the relations between the colonists and the Mexican Government.

Events moved rapidly thereafter, as the slightest incident became a conflict. In February, 1831, Colonel John David Bradburn arrested Land Commissioner Francisco Madero at Anahuac for theoretically overlapping Bradburn's authority. Madero had been instructed to issue land titles to the settlers between Nacogdoches and the Sabine River. Therefore, contrary to Austin's advice, most of the colonists involved themselves by supporting Madero. Mexican Customs Collector George Fisher complicated matters by returning to Texas and also establishing himself at Anahuac. Texas merchants in the colonies were thus faced with having to limit or cease their contraband trade with the United States. A shooting incident at Brazoria in December, 1831, and Fisher's busy-body personality finally prompted General Manuel Miér y Terán to remove Fisher from office. Bradburn, meanwhile, continued to antagonize the situation with his autocratic actions, which led to the arrest of Patrick C. Jones. William B. Travis and others tried to intimidate Bradburn into releasing Jones by playing a practical joke on the commander. The joke backfired and Travis and his friends were arrested. After all legal means had failed, a volunteer company numbering approximately 100 men marched on Anahuac to demand the release of the prisoners. A short skirmish ensued, and the Texans were forced to retreat to Turtle Bayou. In light of the possible implications of their activities, the Texans then issued a resolution emphasizing that they were not rebelling against Mexico, but simply declaring in favor of Santa Anna's *Plan de Vera Cruz.*

The *Plan,* accredited to Antonio López de Santa Anna, sought the overthrow of President Bustamante and his government. Colonel Piedras from Nacogdoches then marched on Anahuac to confer with the Texans and managed to release Jones and Travis on July 3, 1832.

Having become partially involved in national politics by necessity, the Texans decided on August 22 to call a convention to be held October 1, 1832, at San Felipe de Austin. The Texans formally expressed their support for Santa Anna at the convention and asked for the repeal of the anti-colonization clause of the Law of April 6, 1830. They also asked for a reduction of tariff rates, educational and judicial improvements, and separate statehood for Texas.

The convention proceeded to elect Stephen Austin and Erasmo Seguín to carry the petitions to Mexico City. Austin traveled alone and met first with Vice-President Gomez Farias, who promised nothing. Austin later met with President Santa Anna who denied separate statehood for Texas, but managed to repeal the anti-colonization clause of the Law of April 6, 1830. Santa Anna also promised to use his personal influence in procuring the necessary reforms sought by the Texans. Austin left Mexico City on December 3, 1833, but was arrested at Saltillo the following third of January for having advised the City Council of San Antonio to head the movement for separate statehood. He was returned to the capital and imprisoned until December 25, 1834, but was unable to leave Mexico until July 11, 1835. Returning to Texas by way of New Orleans, Austin concluded that war between Texas and the National Government was inevitable.

Meanwhile, the State of *Coahuila y Tejas* had become riddled with factions of federalists, centralists, neutralists, and secessionists. The Constitutional State Assembly meeting at Monclova on June 24, 1834, passed a resolution refusing to recognize Santa Anna as President of Mexico. The Assembly also prepared to raise a militia to defend the Federal Institution. The Coahuila centralists responded on July 19 by establishing their own State Government at Saltillo and declaring all acts of the Monclova Assembly null and void. After much deliberation, Santa Anna solved the problem in December, 1834, by recognizing Monclova and calling for a special election.

Already confused, if not angered, by National and State politics, the Texans met a new crisis in January, 1835, with the arrival at Anahuac of Captain Tenorio, who reopened the military garrison and introduced the new customs collector, Gonzalez. Merchant Andrew Briscoe, irritated with Gonzalez, played an unsuccessful practical joke on the official which caused him to be jailed. News of the incident reached San Felipe de

Austin as a military courier was arriving with a pouch of confidential communiques. The excited Texans promptly confiscated the mail pouch and learned that General Martín P. Cos was preparing to reinforce Tenorio, and that the troops which had crushed the Zacatezan uprising were also being sent to Texas.

Contrary to the wishes of most of the colonists, William B. Travis, leading a group of 25 men, appeared before Anahuac on June 29, 1835, to demand its surrender. Captain Tenorio capitulated the following day and promised to leave Texas. General Cos, upon learning of the incident, ordered Colonel Ugartechea to arrest Travis, R. M. Williamson, and the others involved. By mid-July, however, most Texans of all factions expressed a desire for neither a conflict with nor a separation from the Mexican Government. Thus, after chiding Travis for his impetuous actions, a consultation was scheduled for October 15, 1835, to meet at Washington-on-the-Brazos.

It was amidst this confusion that Austin arrived at Velasco on September 1, 1835. A week later, he addressed a meeting at Brazoria where he repeated his forewarning to Santa Anna that the inevitable consequence of sending troops to Texas would be war. The echo of Austin's words had hardly settled on the Texan countryside when General Martín Perfecto de Cos sailed from Matamoros to Copano Bay. Disembarking on September 21, General Cos proceeded with a small escort to Goliad where he arrived on October 2, as the Texans were dispelling Colonel Ugartechea from Gonzales. Colonel Ugartechea had attempted to recover a small cannon which had been loaned to the citizens of Gonzales for protection against the Indians. Captain Castañeda, the Mexican officer on the field, was defiantly told by the Texans that if he wanted the cannon to "Come and take it." He tried, failed, and retreated to San Antonio.

Cos, meanwhile, continued to San Antonio and arrived on October 9, as a group of Texans under Captain Collinsworth were capturing the fortress and munitions at Goliad. There was no longer any doubt on either side—the Texas Revolution had begun. The outbreak of the revolution found General Cos with a force of 800 men literally besieged at San Antonio. The Texans, encouraged by the victories, hastened to Gonzales and Goliad to create "The Army of the People of Texas." Stephen Austin, elected commander-in-chief of the army, soon directed the force toward San Antonio.

By October 20, the Texan Army had arrived at the Salado Creek Crossing on the Old Goliad Road where a council of war was held. Colonels James Bowie and James Fannin were dispatched thereafter with a

90-man detachment to inspect the lower missions of San Antonio and select a campsite closer to town. The detachment camped in front of Mission Concepcíon on October 27, after reviewing Missions Espada, San Juan and San José. Early the following morning, they were surprised by a Mexican patrol and by 8 a.m. the battle at Concepcíon had begun. The battle ended approximately half an hour later when the Mexican force abandoned the field, leaving some 50 dead and one piece of artillery. The Texans, meanwhile, suffered their first casualty of the revolution, Captain Richard Andrews.

Following a brief council of war, the Texans decided to lay siege to the city and demand a surrender from General Cos. Cos replied, however, that he was duty bound not to capitulate and that he had been ordered to hold San Antonio against all hazards. While fortifying San Antonio, Cos ordered Colonel Ugartechea to Laredo to hurry the expected reinforcements.

In fulfilling their decision to lay siege to the city, the Texans established two encampments. The main camp, commanded by General Stephen Austin, was located directly north of the city along the banks of the San Antonio River. The second camp, commanded by Colonels Bowie and Fannin, remained in the vicinity of Mission Concepcíon. Scouting parties were continuously kept out by the Texans, resulting in the capture of some 300 horses previously sent by Cos to Laredo. The caputred horses were sent to Gonzales to replenish the Texan Army.

Until October 29, when volunteers from East Texas arrived, desertions caused by restless inactivity had been a major problem for the Texans. Although their morale had been temporarily boosted, some colonists, apparently convinced the volunteers would suffice, began to desert to attend to their personal family needs. Another group of volunteers, the "New Orleans Grays," arrived on November 21, and were immediately renamed "The San Antonio Greys."

On the twenty-second of November, Hendrick Arnold and John W. Smith delivered a map showing the Mexican fortifications of San Antonio. Dr. James Grant studied the map and proposed a plan of attack. Austin issued orders for an assault on San Antonio for 3 a.m., November 23. At approximately 1 a.m., however, Lt. Col. Philip Sublett reported to Austin that most of the men opposed the attack. The plan was abandoned after Austin discovered that scarcely 100 men were willing to participate in the assault.

Probably late on November 24, Austin was informed of his appointment by the Provisional Government of Texas as Commissioner to the United States. He gathered the army the following morning to announce his resignation as commander-in-chief of the Texan Army. Edward Burleson was elected to succeed Austin by some 400 men still willing to continue the siege of San Antonio.

On November 26, Texan scout Erastus "Deaf" Smith raced into camp to announce the approach of Colonel Ugartechea and the supposed reinforcements from Laredo. Colonel Bowie and approximately 100 men immediately set out to intercept the Mexican force. The forces met about a mile and a half west of town along a ravine, and a skirmish ensued. As the incident developed into a closely-contested battle, both Generals Cos and Burleson sent reinforcements to their respective forces. By this time the Texans had become aware they were not fighting the long-anticipated reinforcements but a preciously guarded mule caravan instead. The battle continued until the Mexican forces retreated to the security of the town, leaving behind most of the mule cargo. Much to the Texans' surprise, however, the spoils of their victory existed in abundance for everyone except the besieged forces of Genral Cos—grass.

A Texan council of war held on December 3, deliberated attacking the city the following morning but decided, instead, to abandon the siege and establish winter quarters at either Gonzales or Goliad. While preparations for the retreat were being made the following day, a deserting Mexican lieutenant asked to be taken to General Burleson. The lieutenant informed the Texans of the supposedly weak condition of the besieged Mexican forces so Burleson immediately ordered F. W. Johnson and Benjamin R. Milam to call for volunteers. A new hero was born in the ensuing scenes as a loud, clear voice sliced the Texan encampment to ask: "Who will go with old Ben Milam into San Antonio?" "I will," responded some 300 men, and plans for the storming of San Antonio were immediately drawn.

The Texan force was divided into four sections: two assault divisions, one reinforcement unit, and diversionary artillery. The First Assault Division, commanded by Colonel Milam with Major Morris as his aide-de-camp, was to advance southerly along Acequia Street to the de la Garza residence. Scouts for Milam's command were Hendrick Arnold and John W. Smith. The Second Assault Division, commanded by Francis W. Johnson with Colonels John Austin and James Grant as aides-de-camp, was to advance south on Soledad Street and gain possession of the Veramendi House. "Deaf" Smith and Norwich were selected as guides for this command. General Burleson was to remain in camp with the reinforcements while Colonel James C. Neill was to bombard the Alamo in order to create a diversion.

The object of the assault, San Antonio de Béxar, other than being the territorial capital of Texas, was also its religious, military, and socio-economic center. The town itself was composed of four major streets and five *caminos reales*. One of the major north-to-suth streets was Soledad which ran approximately four blocks, from the northern edge of the town past the de la Garza and Veramendi residences to Main Plaza; after passing into Main Plaza it became *Calle de la Quinta*. Also running north to south was *Calle de las Flores* which began about a mile north of town where it branched from the old *Camino Real a San Sabá*. Flores Street then meandered southerly past the Navarro House, the priest's house, the rear of the parish church of San Fernando, and Military Plaza. The street continued on to connect with both the *Camino Real* to Laredo, and Mission Road, both of which led to the lower missions of San Antonio.

The major east-to-west street was known by four distinct names: *Alameda, Potrero, Calle Real,* and *Camino Real al Presidio de Rio Grande*. The street began east of town at the end of the road to Gonzales and continued westwardly past a pecan grove called *Alameda*, from whence it received its name, to the San Antonio River. The section called *Potrero* existed within the horseshoe bend of the river in what used to be the city's old pasture land. *Calle Real* began at Main Plaza and extended westward past the *Acéquia Principal* (main irrigation ditch), Military Plaza, San Pedro Creek, to the cemetery, from when it became the *Camino Real* to Rio Grande. Years later, the four-name thoroughfare would be simplified to East and West Commerce Street. Directly south and parallel to the aforementioned was Dolorosa Street, whose western extremity began on the road to Laredo and ran eastwardly past Military and Main Plazas, and the Ruiz and Seguín homes to the Yturri homestead.

The heart of the town was thus enclosed within the dual-armed cross formed by the four major streets, with the parish church of San Fernando at its center. Most of the houses in this section were of durable *caliche* blocks and had from 18- to 42-inch thick walls. In sharp contrast with the downtown section, were the city's two suburbs of *Laredito* and *La Villita*. Consisting primarily of pallisade shacks and grass huts, *Laredito* lay west of the San Pedro Creek along the Laredo Road. The few stone and mud-pack houses along the street's northern extremity caused it to have another name, "Street of the Little Adobes."

La Villita, officially established in 1809, was located on the east bank of the San Antonio River and was primarily populated with active and retired military personnel. Sweeping northerly from the *Quartel de Béxar* to the Alamo, *La Villita* was composed of stone and *caliche* houses. The abandoned Franciscan mission San Antonio de Valero, commonly known as the Alamo, lay at the northern outskirts of the "little village."

Thus, General Cos' defense of the city consisted of dividing his 800-man force between the Alamo, and Main and Military Plazas. At the Alamo, Cos had placed his artillery and cavalry units. Moreover, he constructed a ramp within the roofless mission church leading from the front door to the rear wall where three artillery pieces were installed. Strategically, though, Cos' defenses at the Alamo were meaningless, as the Texans were to attack the city.

The town defenses, and the apparent objective of the Texans, were the municipal and provincial government offices which were located at the Casas Reales, opposite the east face of Main Plaza. Thus, General Cos placed two barricaded artillery emplacements on the northeast corner of the plaza, facing north on Soledad Street. At the northwest corner of the plaza, opposite Zambrano Row, he installed another artillery emplacement facing north on Acequia Street. Opposite the Navarro House at the northeast corner of Military Plaza, Cos located another artillery emplacement facing north on Flores Street. The Mexican infantry, particularly the sharpshooters, were placed atop the flat-roofed houses along the north side sof the plazas. Command headquarters for the town defenses were apparently established at the residence of Erasmo Seguin, whose house also served as post office.

At dawn, December 5, 1835, Johnson's Second Assault Division emerged from sugar cane fields at the northern limits of the city to march south along the San Antonio River and Soledad Street. The forces then occupied the Veramendi house without difficulty. Five minutes later, Milam's First Assault Division emerged from the same field and marched south along Acéquia Street to the de la Garza house. Before reaching the house, however, a Mexican scout fired upon the division and John W. Smith returned the fire contrary to orders.

Alerted by the exchange of fire, the Mexicans opened fire on the Texans as the latter reached their primary objectives. The doors and windows of the Veramendi and de la Garza houses were secured with timber and sandbags. They also attempted to establish snipers atop the flat roof of the de la Garza house, but the inadequate cover and brisk Mexican fire soon forced them to break holes into the roof and drop to the rooms below. The battle continued until sunset when the opposing forces ceased firing.

Later the first night, General Burleson visited Johnson's Second Division at the Veramendi house. He brought the Texans some beef and found the troops cheerfully enthusiastic. Colonel Johnson then crossed Soledad Street to report to Colonel Milam at the de la Garza house. At the end of the first day, the Texans had lost one man and had six wounded, including Dr. James Grant.

The Texans passed most of the second day in securing and strengthening their positions. Apparently the house adjacent to the Veramendi home on the south was broken into by the Texans where they established an artillery piece directed against the town. A brisk exchange of fire was kept up by both sides, resulting in the wounding of three Texans. The firing ceased at sunset and the Mexicans took advantage of the cover of darkness to install an artillery piece at the Músquiz residence, directly north and adjacent to the Casas Reales. They also established another emplacement on the east bank of the San Antonio River between the Texans' left flank and the Alamo.

December 7, 1835, was a momentous day in the Texas Revolution. Antonio López de Santa Anna, organizing the Mexican Army of Operations at San Luis Potosi for the Texas Campaign, issued orders to General Ramirez y Sesma calling for the giving of no quarter to Texan prisoners. In days to come, he would negate responsibility for this decision and attempt to blame the Mexican National Congress and its decree of December 29, 1835. Still, as President-Dictator of Mexico and Commander-in-Chief of the army on the field, Santa Anna issued the order which prompted the National Congress to pass the decree.

Meanwhile, the fighting at San Antonio continued with the Texans being caught in a crossfire from the Músquiz house and the Mexican artillery located east of the river. Johnson's Second Division was suffering badly when Milam sent his six-pound cannon to assist them. Johnson directed the cannon's fire on the Músquiz house and, with the additional small arms fire, was able to force the Mexicans to abandon their strategic position.

At approximately three thirty that afternoon, Colonel Ben Milam decided to review the Second Division's situation and left the de la Garza house. He raced across Soledad Street and was shot in the head as he entered the Veramendi house. The six-foot commander died instantly, reportedly falling in the arms of Samuel Maverick. He was buried with full military and Masonic honors in the courtyard of the Veramendi house. As the acknowledged leader of the storming of San Antonio, Milam had succeeded in rallying the Texans where Austin and Burleson had failed. Thus, his death gave the Texans an added incentive to continue the fight and avenge his death. Even beyond death, Benjamin Milam aided the Texan cause.

Milam's First Division, now under the command of Major Morris, surged forward to capture the Navarro house, which was opposite the northeast corner of Miiltary Plaza. The Mexican defenders were apparently forced to retreat to the priest's house and to the rear of the parish church of San Fernando. The city's defenses were beginning to fall.

The fighting was somewhat limited the following day due to the cold and wet weather. Yet, the Texans were able to cross Acéquia Street from the Navarro house and capture Zambrano Row. The acquisition of this important house gave the Texans a foothold on the north side of Main Plaza from whence their artillery could command the square. Johnson's Second Division, meanwhile, fought its way from house to house by cutting through the inner walls of the abutting houses while under heavy artillery and musket fire.

The long-awaited Mexican reinforcements escorted by Colonel Ugartechea, but under the command of Colonel Jose Juan Sanchez Navarro, arrived at Bexar on December 9, 1835. Traveling north on Dolorosa Street, the reinforcements arrived at Main Plaza where they were so rapidly distributed that Colonel Sanchez Navarro suddenly found himself alone and without a command. The Colonel could not help but lament the sad assistance being offered by the reinforcements. Not only did the force include conscripted soldiers who had been force-marched from Saltillo to Béxar through the semi-desert extending on either side of Laredo, but they had also been persuaded to do so by the use of chains. The chain gangs had been accompanied by women, children, and merchants who tagged along for reasons best known to themselves.

Colonel Sanchez Navarro, who had not slept for two days, dismounted at the house of Erasmo Seguín and attended to the storing there of the extra shoes, blankets, and hats he had brought. At 11 a.m., the Colonel went to visit General Cos who ordered him an hour later to review the city defenses. After having fired some ineffective shots at the Texans, Colonel Sanchez Navarro retired to the Seguín house where he ate some rice, beans and flour *tortillas* prior to falling asleep. The Colonel was convinced, however, that it was impossible to continue defending the city.

Captain Andres Videgaráy awakened Colonel Sanchez Navarro later that night to announce the battle had been lost because the Texans now controlled the plazas. The Colonel discovered upon inspection that the Texans had moved an artillery piece to the front porch of the priest's house to support their frontal musketry on Main Plaza from Zambrano Row. Valiantly, Colonel Sanchez Navarro joined Colonel Nicolas Condelle in repulsing three charges by the Texans. With sword in hand Sanchez Navarro commanded an artillery piece covering the inch-by-inch retreat of the Mexican infantry. Heavily detrimental to the Mexican cause were the recently arrived reinforcements who, according to Colonel Sanchez Navarro, did not even know how to load a musket, much less fire one. The day ended amidst confusion. Greater confusion occurred that night when entire Mexican cavalry units began to desert en masse.

At 2:45 a.m., December 10, a voice speaking in Spanish sliced across Main Plaza announcing the death of General Cos. The report, however, was fallacious. Colonels Condelle and Sanchez Navarro were at that time commanding an artillery piece in the parochial cemetery, on the south and adjacent to the parish church. Navarro later recorded that he felt his men were like hunted animals being picked off one by one by the Texan sharpshooters. Still, they held their ground until General Cos ordered Sanchez Navarro to join him at the Alamo.

Colonel Sanchez Navarro found a great number of women and children at the Alamo, and much to his surprise, he also discovered some 500 horses eating most of the supplies he had brought from Saltillo. Nonetheless, he presented himself to General Cos who asked the condition of the city's defenses. After hearing the Colonel's report, General Cos ordered him to save whatever men he could, and to begin negotiations for an honorable surrender. Named as his assisting commissioners were José Francisco Rada and the *Jefe Politico,* Ramón Músquiz. Colonel Sanchez Navarro then issued the order for the Mexican troops to cease fire. The Colonel, however, had difficulties convincing his junior officers they should cease firing and honor the wishes of General Cos. He was surrounded by his own men who threatened him at point blank with their muskets, but he reminded them he was merely following orders. Once managing the situation, Colonel Sanchez Navarro lowered the Mexican tri-color and replaced it with a white banner of truce. Accompanied by his commissioners, he then walked to the *Casas Reales* where they were immediately surrounded by Texans.

The Mexican envoys then were taken to Colonel Johnson's headquarters to begin the negotiations. Johnson immediately appointed Robert Morris and James Swisher as his commissioners. The Mexicans then chose Miguel Arciniega as their interpreter; John Cameron was chosen by the Texans. John W. Smith and the parish priest, Refugio de la Garza, soon joined the commissioners. The Texans, however, did not seem in a mood for a parliamentary truce as they coolly reminded the Mexicans they had fired thrice upon Texans carrying a white banner the day before. Moreover, the Mexicans had also flown a black flag near an artillery piece in Main Plaza. The Texans were, apparently, justifiably apprehensive.

General Edward Burleson appeared before the Mexican commissioners and expressed his dissatisfaction that Mexican cavalry units were already leaving the Alamo for the Rio Grande. Actually, the units were deserting General Cos whom they had reportedly trampled in their flight. The negotiations then turned to the political aspects as Sanchez Navarro argued the Mexican forces had not been defeated and, therefore, should not be held as prisoners of war. He concluded he was merely seeking an honorable capitulation favorable to the opposing forces.

At two in the afternoon, the Texans presented eighteen articles of capitulation which were vehemently refused by the Mexican commissioners. Ramón Músquiz saved the situation by noting that the Mexican soldier held personal honor higher than his own life. Músquiz also remained to speak with the Texans after the Mexican commissioners had temporarily left the room. In the course of his conversation, he attempted to show the unreasonable and insulting content of the proposed articles. The heated negotiations continued without avail. Colonel Sanchez Navarro was admittedly worried that the Mexican officers would suffer the same fate as the Spanish officers who had been decapitated in San Antonio by some Texans and insurgent Mexicans in 1813.

At two in the morning of December 11, 1835, the Texans presented eighteen articles of capitulation held agreeable to both sides. The articles began by stating the opposing forces had agreed on the stipulations because they were "desirous of preventing further effusion of blood and the ravages of civil war." Article One dealt with the pardon of General Cos and his officers who were not to oppose, on their word of honor, the re-establishment of the Mexican Constitution of 1824. Cos and the officers did in fact return to fight the Texans, but they did so under the direct command of Santa Anna. Moreover, by the time they returned, the Texans were no longer interested in re-establishing the Mexican Constitution of 1824, but were fighting for independence.

The following eight articles dealt with the disposition of property and the conscripted soldiers, whom the Texans definitely wanted out of the State. The tenth article gave General Cos six days to prepare for the retreat to the Rio Grande. The remaining articles dealt with minor political aspects of the capitulation, such as the protection of people, property and the well being of the sick and wounded.

The commissioners for the opposing forces finally signed the Articles of Capitulation "after a long and serious discussion." The articles were then forwarded to Generals Cos and Burleson who ratified the document with their signatures. General Cos, however, did not delay six days to begin his retreat; he left the following morning at eleven. The departure of the forces under Cos was the turning point in the struggle for Texas independence. Hereafter, all Mexican troops in Texas would be invaders, not defenders, and Texas was destined to remain Texan evermore.

Years later, the companions of Benjamin R. Milam remembered their fallen leader. They returned to the patio of the Vermendi House and recovered the remains of the hero of the storming of Bexar. They disinterred his remains and re-buried them in the old cemetery which later came to be known as Milam Square in San Antonio. A century later, the State of Texas, as well as the Texas Historic Landmarks Association, erected granite markers to honor the memory of Milam and the Minutemen who fought under him.

The Republic of Texas

1836 - 1845

The Signing of the Texas Declaration of Independence -- March 2, 1836

The Texas
Declaration of Independence

By

Rupert N. Richardson

The question of independence became paramount for Texans on February 1, 1836, the day the voters chose delegates to represent them in a convention that would assemble a month later, pass on the subject of independence and deal with other matters exceedingly important and urgent.

In the old East Texas town of Nacogdoches there was excitement and threat of violence that day. On the day before fifty-two Kentucky volunteers had arrived, troops that had been enlisted by Sidney Sherman of Cincinnati who had sold his factory for making cotton bagging and used the money to equip a company to fight in Texas. When the volunteers presented themselves to vote and were refused by the judges, they became furious. Their commander, Lieutenant Woods (Sherman had been detained at Natchitoches by illness), swore that the men would vote or he would "riddle the door" of the polling place with bullets. The crowd of volunteers and citizens was addressed by the candidates, among them Robert Potter, ex-congressman from North Carolina, a man who would have a share in any row in reach and might start one if none were in progress.

Potter, a champion of Texas independence, urged that the volunteers vote. If they had come all the way from Kentucky to fight for Texas, they certainly had a right to help shape its destiny at the polls, he argued. William Fairfax Gray, a genteel Virginian on a visit to Texas to buy land, addressed the volunteers and urged that they not vote. He pointed out that by the terms of the resolution passed by the General Council of the Provisional Government of Texas under which the election was held, it was exceedingly doubtful that troops or other persons who had just arrived from another state had the right to vote. Soldiers were not supposed to take part in political and personal squabbles, he said. But the question was not easily disposed of. The election judges had taken a poll of the citizens and the "Constitutionalists," those who favored continuing as a part of Mexico and fighting for the restoration of the Mexican Constitution of 1824, outvoted the "Independents" by some thirty votes. Since the volunteers were solidly for independence, they had lost in the contest thus far. Both sides were of a wavering will, however: later the judges announced that the volunteers might vote, the volunteers agreed unanimously that they would not vote, then changed their decision and every man voted. Mr. Gray changed his mind and voted too.

The Revolution then under way stemmed from developments of the last decade and even earlier, and the events that brought it about must be given brief notice. Although the twenty thousand Anglo-American colonists in Texas had fared well under the Mexican government, which empresario Stephen F. Austin had pronounced "the most liberal and munificent" on earth, there had been intermittent clashes. In Nacogdoches, disputes between colonists, or would-be colonists, and the old settlers led to an insurrection by the late-comers and their expulsion from the Mexican Nation in 1826-1827. Three years later, fear of the increasing number and growing strength of these Anglo-Americans who, one Mexican averred "carried their political constitution in their pockets," caused the Mexican government to enact and enforce a law that prohibited further colonization of Texas by people from the United States. An indirect result of the law was a formidable insurrection in 1832 that began with an imbroglio between citizens and the commander of troops at Anahuac on Galveston Bay.

Fortunately in this disturbance the Texas colonists linked their cause with that of Antonio López de Santa Anna, the professed liberal who was leading a revolution against President Anastacio Bustamante's government. Santa Anna won, became master of Mexico, and the Texans not only escaped the wrath of the government for the resistance to central authority, but secured the repeal of the offensive law of April 6, 1830, and got other concessions from both the government of Mexico and that of the State of Coahuila and Texas. Notwithstanding a measure of concern over the imprisonment in Mexico City of Stephen F. Austin, their recognized leader, for a political offense, Texans were enjoying peace and prosperity. Each family had been given some forty-four hundred acres of land, taxes were light, and population was increasing rapidly.

The season of satisfaction changed to one of fear and discontent, however, when Santa Anna threw aside his protestations of liberalism, remade the government of Mexico along autocratic lines, and despotically set out to crush all resistance by force of arms. Notable was his defeat of the forces of Zacatecas, which had defied him, and the flaying of that relatively prosperous commonwealth. Through his brother-in-law, Martin Perfecto Cós, Santa Anna overthrew the state government of Coahuila and Texas and arrested Governor Agustín Viesca.

Many Texans, however, viewed Santa Anna's blows at freedom with mixed emotions. The state government had squandered title to millions of acres of land and had become very unpopular. Furthermore, an unseemly protracted quarrel between the Coahuila towns of Saltillo and Monclova over which should be the state capital had caused many Texans to breathe a curse against both places.

Texans did not offer any resistance to Santa Anna until the summer of 1835, when they discovered that he was directing formidable military forces to San Antonio and other points. Even then when William Barrett Travis, in an effort to start a resistance movement, led a small force and captured the garrison at Anahuac, there were more Texan voices of protest than of approval. The peace party was more vocal and probably was in the majority. The political chief at San Felipe (head of one of the three major political divisions of Texas) sent messages of apology with assurances that Travis' act did not have the approval of the rank and file of Texans. Representative groups in several different communities expressed themselves in similar fashion.

But Cós, representing Santa Anna, and his subordinate officer Ugartechea were obdurate. This time the Texans would not get off with mere words of apology as they had in 1832, they must bring forth fruits mete for repentance. Let them arrest and turn over to the Mexican military for trial for treason the noted Mexican liberal now in Texas, Lorenzo de Zavala, Travis, and a few other disturbers of the tranquility. The Mexican demands were refused. Even if he had wished to do so, the political chief could not have imprisoned his fellow Texans; their countrymen would have fought for their release. Now meetings were being held in different communities, other committees of public information were being formed, militia companies were being readied for "defense against the Indians," and a framework for the resistance of tyranny was appearing. The people of Columbia held a meeting and called for a Consultation of representatives of the various localities.

Independence or continuing in the Mexican Republic and cooperating with the liberals of northern Mexico was the issue before the Consultation, which started its work on November 3. The war party, led by Henry Smith and John A. Wharton, favored an immediate and unqualified declaration of independence. The opposition, or peace party, guided by Don Carlos Barrett, Sam Houston, and indirectly by Stephen F. Austin who was commanding troops in the field, opposed a declaration of independence and hoped to gain the support of Mexican liberals by declaring for the Constitution of 1824. Although the peace party won by a vote of 33 to 15, the decision of the assembly and the logic of events during the weeks that followed were against it. The declaration of causes for taking up arms which the Consultation adopted pointed to independence. The body held it to be their right "during the disorganization of the Federal System and the reign of despotism, to withdraw from the Union," but would continue faithful to the Mexican government so long as that nation was governed by the Constitution and laws in conformity with it. The Constitution had been set aside and the nation was not being governed by law.

The Consultation sent Stephen F. Austin, Branch T. Archer, and William H. Wharton to the United States to secure aid, did what it could to strengthen the Texan forces then besieging San Antonio, and manifested in various ways a determination to resist tyranny. It established a provisional government for Texas to consist of a governor, lieutenant governor, and general council of one member from each municipality. A hastily written instrument setting forth the powers and plan of the provisional government was unsatisfactory. The governor, Henry Smith, and the council quarreled over their respective authority and the government soon became divided and almost impotent. It did, however, hold together long enough to call a Constitutional Convention, the delegates to be elected by the people and "clothed with ample, unlimited, or plenary powers as to the form of government to be adopted: *provided,* that no Constitution formed shall go into effect, until the same be submitted to the people and confirmed by a majority thereof." The resolution calling the Convention, dated December 10, 1835, did not call for separation from Mexico, but its tenor was warlike. It advocated "courage and bravery in resistance," and stated that "arms are the resort, and in arms the people will find their only security from the oppression of ambitious tyrants." It is significant that on the day this resolution was adopted Texas troops forced the capitulation of Cós and a thousand troops and took over San Antonio.

Talk of independence was heard on every hand. At Goliad on December 20, two old Texans, Ira Ingram and Philip Dimmitt, framed a Declaration of Independence, declaring "that the former province and department of Texas is, and of a right ought to be, *a free, sovereign and independent state.*" Read to the citizens of Goliad, the document was enthusiastically ratified and signed by ninety-one citizens. Copies were sent out, one to Brazoria that was widely distributed. The General Council of the Provisional Government, however, regarded it as an untimely hindrance. The body was negotiating with José Antonio Mexia, the Mexican liberal, in the vain hope of securing aid from the north Mexican federalists.

Pursuant to the terms of the resolution of December 10 enacted by the provisional government, the seventeen municipalities and "the Citizens of Pecan Point," as that region was designated, held elections on February 1, 1836. Apparently voting was orderly in most communities and there were few contests except in matters pertaining to voting by non-resident soldiers. The excitement in Nacogdoches has been noted already. We have seen that the volunteers there finally did vote and it should be added that their votes elected the fiery champion of independence, Robert Potter. His vote was 235, the lowest of the four delegates chosen, and just three more than that of John K. Allen.

The question of the right of troops to vote apparently arose wherever troops happened to be located on election day. The judges at Refugio refused to permit 177 soldiers stationed there to vote. Whereupon the troops held their own election and chose from their ranks David Thomas and Edward Conrad to represent them. At San Patricio the troops were apparently not permitted to vote, but their candidate, John White Bower, was seated over his opponent, John McMullen, after it was brought out that the troops were for Bower. Claims of Samuel Rhoads Fisher to a seat in the Convention were sustained on the ground that, although his opponent, Richard R. Royall, received a few more votes, Royall's total had been augmented by the votes of volunteers who had been discharged some weeks before. At Velasco, in the Municipality of Brazoria, the election officers listed the names of eighty-eight men who voted, at least forty-seven of whom had been recruited in New Orleans for the Texas army and had been in Texas only four days. Every man of the eighty-eight listed voted for James Collinsworth, a staunch champion of independence. The report showed that at least 188 other men had voted by proxy.

The citizens of Bexar Municipality (San Antonio), who had hitherto taken but little interest in the conventions of Texas, elected four delegates to represent them in the forthcoming Convention. Only two of these, Francisco Ruiz and J. Antonio Navarro, attended. When the volunteers in Bexar were denied the right to vote by the resident election judges because they were not residents of Bexar, their commander, Colonel J. C. Neill, ordered an election to be held in the Alamo and two soldiers were elected to represent the troops. Thus it was that a few days later Jesse B. Badgett and Samuel A. Maverick, at the behest of their comrades, rode away from San Antonio and escaped the sad fate of their fellow soldiers when the Alamo fell on March 6.

Badgett carried with him a petition signed by the officers at Bexar, setting forth the facts and requesting that he and Maverick be seated. The petition was in forceful and convincing language. Volunteers and regular soldiers had been declared citizens by the Consultation and thereby given the right to vote. The election judges at Bexar had ruled that only citizens of Bexar could vote. "Yet a large portion of this army," the petition read, "do not yet possess any local habitation whatsoever." The petition continued by pointing out that it was important that men of the army represent the army, and it added that the Mexican people of San Anonio joined with the troops in wishing representation for the troops. Badgett and Maverick were seated without question.

An index to the practices of the Texans, illustrating how they were determined to enlist in their cause every man who might wish to join them, may be found in their dealings with Pecan Point, the vicinity in extreme northeast Texas. These settlers, some of whom had preceded in coming to Texas by several years the earliest resident of Austin's colony, had not previously taken part in Texas affairs. The boundary line had been designated by the treaty of 1819 between Spain and the United States but it had not been fixed. These people resided mainly in Miller County, Arkansas, which later tourned out to include a broad strip of North Texas. The resolution of the provisional government calling the Convention gave these people the nod of recognition when it named the seventeen Texas municipalities with the number of delegates to be allowed each, and closed with the phrase, "and the citizens of Pecan Point two." Pecan Point originally applied to a small settlement on the north side of Red River, but by 1835 it had come to include much of the present Fannin, Lamar, Red River, and Bowie counties.

But now that their interest was turned toward Texas, the citizens of Pecan Point were not satisfied with representation just as if they were one municipality and sending two delegates to the Convention. They seized time by the forelock and on January 27, 1836, election judges, writing at the home of Collin McKinney, reported for the "Municipality of Red River" (no such municipality had been created) the names of five men to represent the municipality in the Convention. They had chosen good men and true: Collin McKinney, wise with his seventy years; Robert Hamilton, the wealthiest man who would attend the Convention; Samuel Price Carson, who had been for eight years a congressman from North Carolina; Richard Ellis, who would be chosen to preside over the Convention; and James H. Johnson. These men, except Johnson who did not attend the Convention, were seated without contest. Pecan Point and vicinity still had another representative in the Washington, Texas meeting. Albert Latimer appeared before the committee on elections and asked to be seated on the grounds that the region was entitled to six representatives. It was not then known that Johnson would not claim his seat. Latimer did not say that he had been elected but the committee approved him and the Convention, apparently following the credo that it could not have too many good men or too much good will, seated him.

The Pecan Point delegation was indeed unique. Although Johnson did not attend, with Latimer the delegation was larger than that of any other jurisdiction. All five of the delegates claimed to be residents of Arkansas and none of them had received any land from the Spanish or Mexican governments. L. W. Kemp, the authority on the subject, states that it is doubtful if Carson was at any time prior to March 2, 1836, even technically a citizen of Texas. His residence was either in North Carolina or Arkansas and he was a citizen of one or the other of those states. But Texas needed men, and Texas could make good use especially of a man of the stature of Samuel Price Carson.

Although the Conventions of 1832 and 1833 and the Consultation of 1835 had drawn their attention to the course of public affairs and acquainted them with some men who had the capacity for leadership, Texas voters were handicapped by the slender circulation of newspapers and their lack of acquaintance with one another and with the candidates. Over half the candidates elected had been in Texas less than five years and the majority of the voters likewise were newcomers. Still, on that February day in 1836 the voters did very well in selecting men to represent them in a gathering that was destined to change the course of history. From their own ranks they chose men who typified quite faithfully the various facets of Texas society and represented their sentiments and common interests.

The men selected were mainly from the old South: twelve of the fifty-nine natives of Virginia; ten natives of North Carolina; and nine of Tennessee. Most of them were young men in their thirties (Edward Conrad, the youngest, was twenty-five). Still, age was not unrepresented. James Gaines, sixty, had known Texas since the days of the Neutral Ground agreement in 1806, had invaded the land with filibusters in 1812 and 1813, when it was a Spanish territory. He was first alcalde of the District of Sabine in 1824; and had helped to suppress the Fredonian Rebellion in 1826-1827. The thrifty, Scotland-born bachelor, Robert Hamilton, who became a Red River planter of considerable wealth, was about fifty-eight. Later he served the Republic of Texas on an important mission to the United States. Mention has been made of the Nestor of the body, Collin McKinney, known to his neighbors as "Squire" McKinney, seventy. His influence in the Convention must have been considerable. He was a member of the First, Second, and Fourth Congresses of the Republic of Texas, and before death overtook him in 1861 he had outlived a majority of his companions in the Convention.

Among a people many of whom lived and traveled in the peril of attack by marauding Indians, it was consistent that the Indian trade be represented. Born in Canada, the former trapper, Indian trader, and Indian chief, Michael B. Menard, who had learned to speak English after he had migrated to Illinois as a young adult, moved to Texas about 1829. At Nacogdoches he traded for some time with Indians and Mexicans. Later he laid out the town of Galveston and served in the Fifth Congress of the Republic of Texas. He was a Catholic and a Mason.

Martin Parmer was born in Virginia in 1778, migrated to Missouri and hunted and trapped in what is now Carroll County. After numerous adventures and fights with Indians he gained great influence over them and later was Indian agent. His frontier life is reflected in his sobriquet "The Ringtailed Panther" which he seemed to like. The historian Henderson Yoakum apparently gave credence to the anecdote that while on the frontier Parmer sent fifty miles for a preacher for the funeral of his prized bear-dog, and supposing that it was a member of the Parmer family, the clergyman attended. Moving to Texas, Parmer took part in the Fredonain Rebellion, 1826-1827, and on its failure retired across the Sabine. He returned to Texas to make his home in 1835 and was elected to the Consultation and the Convention.

The pioneering background of the delegates was not confined to former trappers, traders, and others who had dealt directly with Indians. Reports of delay and concern over Indian maraudings were not uncommon at the Convention. No doubt others traveled after the fashion of the lawyer Albert Hamilton Latimer who rode a mule on his four hundred-mile trip from the Pecan Point settlements to Washington-on-the-Brazos, taking with him a bag of parched corn and depending on his rifle for meat.

Several different professions were represented in the body. In the list of doctors was Junius William Mottley, who had "read" medicine under Dr. Charles Hay, father of the statesman-author John Hay, and spent two years in the medical college of Transylvania University, Lexington, Kentucky. Stephen H. Everitt of New York was a doctor but did not practice medicine in Texas. He was senator from the First through the Fifth Congress of the Republic.

William Carrol Crawford, a Methodist preacher, was a "confirmed dyspeptic, expecting to be buried by the way" when he left Alabama for Texas in 1834, but he lived to be the last surviving member of the Convention and died in 1895. He was related to Charles Carroll, the last surviving signer of the United States Declaration of Independence.

Lawyers were plentiful in the Washington gathering. Probably some of them had only a slender practice or none at all and looked to other work or interests for a living. George C. Childress, a Nashville lawyer and for some time one of the editors of *The Nashville Banner* and *Nashville Advertiser,* used his newspaper to promote meetings and raise funds and troops for the Texas cause, and for a period probably did more for Texas than any other United States resident. He came to Texas in 1835, was elected to the Convention from the Municipality of Milam and is credited with writing the Declaration of Independence. Childress also introduced the resolution that made "a single star of five points, either of gold or silver . . . the peculiar emblem of this republic."

James Collinsworth, another Tennessee lawyer, was United States district attorney for a period before he migrated to Texas in 1835. He became an aggressive champion of the war party and took an active part in meetings that led to the Revolution. He apparently was influential on the judiciary committee of the Convention and his conduct at the Battle of San Jacinto drew high praise from General Houston. Later he was acting secretary of state, represented Texas to the government of the United States, and was a member of the First Senate of the Republic of Texas.

The South Carolinian, Thomas Jefferson Rusk, a friend of John C. Calhoun's, moved to Georgia and acquired a lucrative law practice. After unscrupulous managers had absconded with the property of a mining and land speculating company in which he had invested heavily, he felt impelled to follow them to Texas and try to recover some of the funds. In this effort he failed, but he became a Texan and in the course of time attained renown. He was an officer in the Texas army, was active in the Constitutional Convention, was secretary of war of the ad interim government, a member of the Congress of the Republic, and a United States senator.

The relatively few Texans of renown and political experiences were well represented in the Convention. Virginia-born Richard Ellis had been a member of the Alabama constitutional convention of 1819 and a judge of the supreme court of that state before he moved to the Pecan Point country, then known as Miller County, Arkansas. Late in 1835 he was elected to represent Miller and Sevier counties in a constitutional convention to meet at Little Rock, but he did not attend and resigned the position. A little later he appeared at Washington, Texas, with credentials indicating that the voters of Pecan Point and vicinity had chosen him to represent them in the Texas Constitutional Convention and was elected president of that body. The reason for Ellis' selection to this high post is not clear. James Collinsworth stated later that when he arrived at Washington on March 1 it "seemed to be understood that Richard Ellis from that part of Red River under the Conventional jurisdiction of the United States was to be president," and that he was chosen without opposition. The fact that Ellis had served in one constitutional convention, had been elected to a second, and now to a third may account for his selection as president. Another factor must be given notice, however. Texans evidently were appealing to the Miller County, Pecan Point people, who had as late as the summer of 1835 considered themselves citizens of Arkansas. We have seen that the general council had allowed "the citizens of Pecan Point" two representatives, that the citizens insisted on having more and elected five, and that four of the five were seated. It will be recalled also that Latimer, who had not been elected, was seated before it was known that Johnson, one of the five who had been elected, would not claim his seat. There were many hundreds of these Red River pioneers and Texas needed the help of every one of them.

Eight years in Congress and attendance on the North Carolina constitutional convention of 1835 had given Samuel Price Carson greater legislative experience than any other member. It will be recalled that he too was from Pecan Point and vicinity and that his home actually was in Arkansas or North Carolina. His activities were curtailed because he did not enter the Convention until March 10. He was secretary of state for a period and later represented the interests of Texas in Washington. Kemp states that Carson expended a sizable portion of his fortune in behalf of Texas.

Robert Potter, the former congressman from North Carolina has already been introduced. He is perhaps best remembered in the Convention for his proposal after a stirring message had been received from Travis on March 6, that a committee of five be appointed to serve as a provisional government and that "the Convention adjourn to meet in the camp of our countrymen, there or elsewhere to complete the business of the govt." A debate followed and fortunately the motion lost. The body followed a wiser course in sending Sam Houston into the field to take command of the meager armed forces that had to reckon with Santa Anna's thousands of invading troops. Potter served as ad interim secretary of the navy and was a member of the Fifth and Sixth Congresses. He was killed in a feud in 1842.

Three native Mexicans were members of the Convention. José Antonio Navarro, of Bexar, had served in the Mexican Congress, and José Francisco Ruiz, also of Bexar, was later a member of the Texas Congress. Lorenzo de Zavala, a native Mexican, well known on two continents, had been deputy to the first Mexican Congress, president of the Congress that had written the Mexican Constitution of 1824, senator, governor of the state of Mexico, secretary of the treasury, and minister to Paris. After Santa Anna discarded all pretense of constitutional government, de Zavala broke with him, retired to Texas, was active in the Constitutional Convention of 1836 and was elected vice-president of the ad interim Texas government.

Perhaps the best known individual in Texas at that time was Sam Houston, a friend of Andrew Jackson, former member of Congress, and governor of Tennessee. His political experience and skill at winning votes enabled him to be elected to represent the Municipality of Nacogdoches in the Convention of 1833 and the Consultation of 1835. His popularity had waned greatly, however, during the winter of 1835-1836, when as the titular commander of the Texas army he had been able to accomplish so little, and he was defeated decidedly in his home Municipality of Nacogdoches in the election of February 1. The troops at Refugio also rejected him as their delegate. We have seen that the citizens of Refugio elected him. The discerning Virginian William Fairfax Gray gave Houston a place in his diary. "Houston's arrival at the Convention created more sensation than that of any other man," he wrote and added that "he seems to take pains to ingratiate himself with everybody." It may be repeated that Houston was elected by the Convention to be commander-in-chief of the Texas Army and on March 6 he left for the field.

Discomforts and inconveniences at San Felipe, hitherto the chief center of government of Anglo-American Texas, accounted in part for the selection of the new town of Washington, some fifty miles up the Brazos, as the meeting place for the Convention. Even so, one wonders if the change brought much improvement, especially in view of the fact that there was no printing press at Washington. The house where the meetings were held belonged to Noah T. Byars, later widely known as a Baptist preacher, and his business partner, Peter M. Mercer. It was rented by the owners to a committee of Washington merchants who tendered it free of charge to the Convention. The building had not been finished: windows had not been inserted, and cotton cloth nailed over the openings only helped a little to keep out the wind when the group convened with the mercury at thirty-three degrees. A visitor described the setting thus: "A long rough table extended from near the front door to near the rear wall, and was equidistant from the side walls. On this table the public documents and the papers of the Convention were laid and the delegates were seated around it, the presiding officer sitting at the end and the secretary nearest him on his left. There was no bar around this table to prevent intrusion upon deliberations. . . . Spectators entered the chamber at will, but they walked gently so as not to annoy the delegates."

It is stated that at the time of the Convention the new town had two hotels, fifty houses, and about a hundred inhabitants. On his visit to the place shortly before the delegates gathered, W. F. Gray "stopt at a house called a tavern," the only place where he could get fodder for horses. The frame house, consisting of one room forty by twenty feet, was heated by a large fireplace at each end. "A blackguard, rowdy set were lounging about," Gray related' and added: "The host's wife and children, and about thirty lodgers, all slept in the same apartment, some in beds, some on cots, but the greater part on the floor. The supper consisted of fried pork and coarse corn bread and miserable coffee."

But in spite of the unpromising setting, the men who assembled in Washington-on-the-Brazos that cold March morning in 1836 had determination and a pronounced sense of urgency. Indeed they had cause to have, for they knew that a hundred and fifty miles to the west Santa Anna's legions were closing in on Travis' little band in the Alamo and they must have conjectured that a contingent of cavalry could leave San Antonio, reach Washington in three or four days, and make the last one of them prisoners. There were frequent rumors and reports of such a Mexican advance, and before they finished their work they had many alarms and excursions.

Their accomplishments were stupendous. Probably no deliberative body in history ever did more in so short a period—seventeen days. Ahead of them was the task of deciding the question of independence, framing a Constitution to be ratified by the voters after the enemy had been beaten and a semblance of order restored, and of establishing a strong government ad interim for the emergency. These tasks were great, but far more burdensome was the work of setting the course of public affairs in order and taking steps to win the Revolution. While the Convention endured, it was the government of Texas and on the whole it did its work well. Let us keep in mind, however, that this narrative is confined mainly to the declaring of independence.

The body had little time for the routine of organization. James Collinsworth was chosen temporary chairman, credentials were examined, Richard Ellis was elected president and H. S. Kimble, a Tennesseean who was not a member, was made secretary. Without delay and pursuant to a resolution that there should be a committee on a Declaration of Independence, President Ellis appointed George C. Childress, James Gaines, Edward Conrad, Collin McKinney, and Bailey Hardeman to write the instrument and report. Childress was chosen chairman of the committee and it has been generally assumed that he wrote the document, or the greater part of it, and that the other members approved it with little change. In fact, the tradition that he brought it with him to the Convention seems plausible in view of the very short time that the committee had the matter before it. A newspaper editor, Childress was the one experienced writer on the committee.

The committee submitted its report on the following day, March 2; the convention resolved itself into a committee of the whole; Sam Houston made a "declamatory" speech; and the Declaration of Independence was accepted without change and turned over to the engrossing clerks.

The opposition to a Declaration of Independence had been strong and persistent. We have seen that the Consultation in the preceding November refused to make such a declaration. The idea of seeking the aid of Mexican liberals to restore constitutional government in Mexico had a forceful appeal to the rank and file of conservative Texans. Mention has been made of the fact that the provisional government regarded the Declaration of Independence of the citizens of Goliad as abortive. In the election of February 1 Mexican citizens at Nacogdoches were solidly against independence; and Gray recorded in his diary meeting various Anglo-Americans who were for the Mexican Constitution of 1824 and believed that a satisfactory government could be restored to power under it. In the election none of the citizen voters of the Municipality of Matagorda, in South Texas, favored independence.

But with the advance of Santa Anna's army opposition to independence diminished rapidly. On March 3, all members present signed the Declaration of Independence as presented by Childress and his committee; late-comers signed it in due course. Gray reported that two Nacogdoches members, John S. Roberts and Charles S. Taylor, expressed some "difficulty" about signing, but finally added their names.

Five copies of the Declaration of Independence were despatched forthwith to designated Texas communities and a thousand copies ordered to be printed by the press at San Felipe. The original was deposited with the United States Department of State in Washington, D. C. and was not returned to Texas until near the end of the century. On March 2, 1930, the historic document was placed in the State Archives in Austin and a photographic copy enshrined in the Capitol.

The Declaration begins with a statement of the innate right of a people to abolish a government that has "ceased to protect the lives, liberty, and property of the people, from whom its legitimate powers are derived," has discarded constitutional government and become a "consolidated central military despotism." Then follow more than a dozen allegations against the Mexican government or the Mexican nation. These charges may be grouped in three categories: specific unjust acts, omissions, and general allegations. Among the specific acts were listed the imprisonment of Austin in Mexico without trial; abuses of garrison troops in the communities where they were stationed; demands for the surrender of citizens to the military for trial; breaking up the government of Coahuila and Texas; piratical attacks on Texas commerce; invasion of the country by land and sea; and inciting Indians to commit depredations. There is some foundation in history for each of these charges.

Among the allegations or omissions of the Mexican government, its failure to act, are set forth its failure to establish a public school system; its denial of freedom of religion; its failure to provide for trial by jury; and its failure to grant Texas separate statehood. These allegations are not without foundation, but some of them invite rebuttal. It is true that the Mexicans had not provided a public school system, but neither did the Republic of Texas or the State of Texas in an early day, except in a very meager fashion. In respect to religious freedom it may be noted that a start had been made in the state law of 1834 providing a measure of religious toleration. A court system with jury trial had been set up for Texas. It did not function satisfactorily, but the defects could have been remedied.

The general allegations in the Declaration of Independence against the Mexican government and the Mexican nation were well stated. Among these were the refusal to permit separation from Coahuila; the overthrowing of the federal system of government by Santa Anna and the acquiescing of the Mexican nation in these changes; and the fact that "during the whole time of our connection with it [the Mexican government had been] the contemptible sport and victim of military revolutions, and hath continually exhibited every characteristic of a weak, corrupt, and tyrannical government."

It was a fact that union with Coahuila made state government exceedingly expensive and difficult for Texans. Santa Anna's tyranny had become an ominous threat to all freedom, and revolution had been almost the normal state of things for Mexico during the years Texans had known it. For a decade they had kept out of these imbroglios, but in recent years they had been caught up in them. To avoid them they must separate from Mexico.

The men in the Convention at Washington-on-the-Brazos did not secure Texas independence, but they declared it effectively and made possible its realization. Amidst terrifying reports of destruction and death wrought to the slender Texas arms and with their own lives in peril, these champions of freedom stayed at their task until they had assured the Revolution more stamina, had strengthened the cause of Texas abroad, and under sturdy President David G. Burnet had set up a government ad interim that could prevent anarchy.

Meanwhile Sam Houston had proceeded to Gonzales and taken command of a slender band of troops. Here he began a retreat until the addition of volunteers and better organization and discipline had given him a force equal to the task that was his. When at San Jacinto, on April 21, 1836, Houston attacked and destroyed the spearhead of Santa Anna's armies, the dream of independence, so dear to the men at Washington-on-the-Brazos, became a reality.

The United States

1846 - 1861

The Annexation of Texas to the Union -- February 19, 1846

From Republic to State:
The Annexation of Texas

By

BEN H. PROCTER

Just before midnight on March 3, 1837, a tall rough-hewn man, his white hair combed but still magnificently unruly, his rugged face a reflection of dominance and command, signed a document before him. Then he turned to two interested friends from Texas, William H. Wharton and Memucan Hunt, and invited them to toast the occasion with a glass of wine. Although he had delayed official government action for almost a year (after all, the United States had treaty obligations with Mexico), now the deed was done. President Andrew Jackson had recognized Texas as an independent Republic.

Yet this action failed to please any of the parties involved. From first mention in 1836, Democrats who favored Martin Van Buren for President had scorned the suggestion of annexation or recognition of independence, fearful that by taking either stand they would lose votes for their candidate among Northern abolitionists, indeed that they would acquire the mark of political lepers. Even Jackson had hesitated, although hating the Mexicans and obviously admiring the courage of his old comrade-in-arms Sam Houston. When asked about recognizing the new Republic, he forestalled the answer by sending Henry M. Morfit there as an observer of "civil, military and political conditions"--and not until this State Department clerk reported his findings would he consider making a judgment. At the same time Secretary of State John Forsyth proved to be unusually aloof and discouraging, often unreceptive to anything Texan. When Wharton arrived in Washington and called upon him late in December, 1836, he icily suggested that Texas should "get its first recognition somewhere else." In fact, had it not been for Wharton maneuvering adeptly and skillfully, Jackson might not have agreed in January, 1837, to abide by Congressional action on the subject. Consequently, with the Senate Foreign Relations Committee asking for Texas recognition as well as a House appropriation for an American diplomatic representative, the President finally acquiesced.

American concern, however, was infinitesimal compared to the outraged feelings of Mexican officials. Vehemently they objected to American recognition of Texas, to sanctioning and comforting outlaws and rebels, those "Diablos Tejanas." What unmitigated gall! How could the United States declare a province joined to Coahuila, although temporarily outside of Mexican authority, as a nation either *de facto* or *de jure*? By extortion those cutthroats had compelled General Antonio López de Santa Anna to grant them independence, that is, until he was released and no longer threatened by their "thirsty Bowie knives." And when Mexican forces might have moved to suppress the rebellion during the summer of 1836, United States troops under General Edmund P. Gaines had interfered, ostensibly seizing Nacogdoches to protect American citizens from Indian raids. Yet no Mexican was fooled by this well-planned ruse, by this conspicuous American scheme to dismember the Mexican empire. First, troops had arrived, disguised as settlers; then to protect and support them, Jackson had stationed Gaines on the Louisiana border; and now that the prospect of annexation was unlikely, he had done the next best thing—recognizing Texas as an independent republic.

Despite this obviously favorable concession by Jackson, Texans also felt aggrieved. What they had desired most was perfectly clear—to join the Union, to become a state among equals, to escape the threat of being conquered by a nation grounded in absolutism and Catholicism. To them, Herbert Gambrell observed, "foreign relations had meant merely putting Texans into the United States which they thought could be done almost overnight." For that matter they equated annexation with recognition of independence. But such rationalizations, they soon found out, were erroneous. In June, 1836, James Collinsworth and Peter W. Grayson, former members of President David G. Burnet's cabinet and now the Texas commissioners to the United States, could do nothing. For instance, Secretary of State Forsyth refused to receive them officially because their credentials were not in order; their commissions, through an oversight, did not contain the Great Seal of the Republic of Texas. Even a national plebiscite in September, wherein only ninety-one voters in all the Republic opposed annexation, did not improve their position or sway Forsyth and Jackson appreciably. If anything, it proved to be a blunder, "greatly embarrassing" to the negotiators. For how could Collinsworth and Grayson accomplish their mission when Van Buren Democrats were pressuring government officials to steer clear of the slavery question? In December after fruitless meetings and frustrating delays, the two Texans left Washington. And only through the manipulations—and luck—of their replacements, Wharton and Hunt, was recognition accomplished.

But what now? Although disappointed, Texans believed that annexation was the next logical step, merely a question of time, a matter which could be achieved by perseverance and diplomacy. To carry out their dreams and expectations they had elected Sam Houston as president. Unquestionably he had the experience, the knowledge, the political know-how—and he would be successful.

No one realized better than Houston what was expected of him. Nor was he or anyone else oblivious to the salutary effects that annexation might have upon him personally. So he pressed for an immediate, successful conclusion. With Wharton having resigned (Forsyth had angered him by not accepting his credentials), Houston appointed General John T. Mason and former minister Peter Grayson, both of whom were skilled and knowledgeable, as added support to the Washington delegation. Then he directed Hunt to consummate "the great and paramount object—Annexation."

Quickly the Texas delegates, now officially recognized by the Van Buren Administration, maneuvered to carry out their instructions. Hunt especially had a grand design. Pressure diplomacy was the answer—play upon American fears; pursue your adversary relentlessly, but keep open all possible channels of communication. On April 15, 1837, he wrote Texas Secretary of State James Pinckney Henderson that, by flirting with the British and acting as if some understanding was imminent, he might persuade "even Northern politicians . . . [to] advocate our connection." Yet after six weeks of this cat and mouse game he realized that Van Buren—and the aloof Forsyth in particular—would not budge so long as Mexico, by protesting and at times threatening war, kept the slavery issue before the American public. In this respect Southern newspapers such as the *New Orleans Picayune,* editorializing that any congressman who tried "to dodge the subject of admitting Texas should be hurled from his seat as a traitor," were equally harmful. So distraught did Hunt become with his situation, so positive in his conviction of what must be done, that on May 30 he advised Henderson: "We must either whip Mexico into an acknowledgement of our independence, or procure . . . recognition by either England or France before we can hope for any definite action . . . by the United States."

Agreeing with this line of diplomacy, President Houston in June appointed Henderson as roving ambassador to England and France, specifically to obtain recognition and enlist financial aid. In turn, Hunt awaited the repercussions of such action, the fears that it might evoke among Americans, the pressures that the Van Buren Administration would soon feel. Then with the time seemingly propitious he implemented his plan. On August 4 he submitted to Secretary of State Forsyth a formal petition for annexation approximately twenty pages in length. After briefly reviewing the historical background of Texas and its method of colonization, he explained the beneficial effects of immediate union. Obviously both countries would profit. The United States would eliminate a possible rival on the continent, would control the Gulf of Mexico as well as acquire vast stretches of fertile lands; on the other hand Texas would elude those extreme difficulties confronting a struggling young nation—the problems of establishing a federal government, of economic self-sufficiency, of frontier defense, of somehow balancing liberty and order. And actually through common heritage, through a basic acceptance of Judeo-Christian beliefs, through a reverence for the Constitution and democratic processes, the people of both countries were already one. Why not make it official?

But Forsyth was a fortress, unyielding and impenetrable. For three weeks he refused to acknowledge Hunt's proposal, much less reply to it. When he did, however, there was no question concerning his stand, no vague generalities or ambiguities. "The United States was bound to Mexico by a treaty of amity and commerce," he announced, and regardless of the "powerful and weighty" arguments for annexation they were "light when opposed in the scale of reason to treaty obligations and respect for . . . integrity of character." Nor would he give credence to other comments that Hunt offered in reply. Previous offers by the United States to buy Texas, he asserted, had nothing to do with present circumstances; annexation might be unconstitutional; President Jackson had been hasty in granting recognition. Still the letters continued between the two men, until in September, 1837, such inflexibility finally discouraged the Texas delegation, Hunt concluding that "it would be derogatory to ourselves to insist upon . . . [annexation] any longer."

In Texas, Doctor Anson Jones, a congressman from Brazoria, agreed wholeheartedly with Hunt; and as far as he was concerned, all negotiations should cease immediately. During the past year American diplomatic conduct had been to him reprehensible, insulting, at best condescending. Whereas Texas had sent a minister plenipotentiary to Washington, the United States had reciprocated with a mere chargé d'affaires. And no matter how logical the arguments for union, no matter the method of approach, the Van Buren Administration had rebuffed every overture.

But no more. The affronts, the discourtesies by the United States were at an end; Jones was going to make sure of that. In the fall of 1837 he proposed in the Texas House of Representatives that the Republic renounce the doctrine of annexation and declare that "no such intention, or wish, exists on the part of the people of this government." To his chagrin the resolution was tabled, but within ten days he moved that

President Houston reduce the rank of the Washington minister to a chargé d'affaires. Before the legislative session ended in December, however, he and his colleagues, becoming increasingly irritated by American attitude, pushed through a measure to recall the Texas delegation as well as the consul in New York.

So in April, 1838, at the last session of the Second Congress the topic of greatest concern, the issue arousing the deepest emotion, was annexation. And once again Dr. Jones was leading the opposition. With newspapers having had a picnic for over a year at Texas' expense, he was "indignant at the position we occupied, and satisfied it was impolitic and unwise in any respect to occupy it longer." After the Senate Foreign Relations Committee recommended on April 17 that the annexation proposal be unconditionally withdrawn," he tried to apply the coup d'grace. On April 23 he presented a joint resolution to the House incorporating the Senate report but which also provided for a certain procedure for President Houston to follow. By one vote his motion was defeated; consequently for the next week his colleagues suggested several amendments, all having the same purpose in mind and all losing by the same slim margin.

Yet Jones, although beaten in these legislative ploys, soon won his case. On June 5 Memucan Hunt officially resigned as minister and left Washington. When Grayson, the most logical successor, refused to take his place, Houston decided to appoint Anson Jones. Specifically instructed by the President to withdraw the annexation proposal, he closed out more than two years of fruitless negotiations on October 12, 1838. Just prior to this final action he enthusiastically exclaimed: "We remain a 'Spunky little independent Republic' with all our blushing honors thick upon us."

Nor at this moment did he fear a reversal of this policy. On December 1, 1838, Mirabeau B. Lamar became President of the Republic—and his views towards annexation were already well known. A move in that direction, he asserted, "would produce a lasting regret, and ultimately prove as disastrous to our liberty and hopes as the triumphant sword of the enemy." Besides, Lamar had conjured up grander, more elaborate schemes which in no way included union. During his term of office he envisioned the beginning of a magnificent Texas empire encompassing endless tracts of land from the Sabine to the Pacific. This policy of expansion would be his gift to the people of Texas, indeed a monument to his administration.

Consequently, for the next three years the annexation issue died from "its own inertia" or, at best, lay dormant. Yet Lamar indirectly revived the question as a result of his administrative policies. An avowed enemy of "Old Sam," he reversed many of Houston's programs. Never could he coddle or respect the Indians, those savages who had massacred and plundered all along the frontier, who had conspired with Mexico to re-enslave Texans, who claimed and resided on lands that were not legally theirs. While Houston had made treaties with various tribes, he favored establishing a line of forts to protect the frontier before embarking upon an extermination campaign. After two years of bloody encounters (1839-1840), the Texans finally subdued their red enemies, particularly the Cherokees and Comanches, one significant result being, however, that the Republic plunged deeper into debt.

Again in regard to Mexico, Lamar was also much more militant and aggressive than Houston. True, on three separate occasions he sent ambassadors to effect a satisfactory understanding. And true, he sought an honorable peace. But with the Mexicans rejecting each mission and with their attitude increasingly hostile, he concluded: "If peace can only be obtained by the sword, let the sword do it." In 1841, however, Congress would not agree to this suggested course of action; it was far too dangerous. So he chose instead to employ less direct but equally provoking tactics. In September, after rebels in the Mexican state of Yucatan had overthrown the government, he signed a treaty of alliance with them. To prevent an invasion by the central government he dispatched Commodore Edwin Ward Moore with the Texas navy to intercept the Mexican fleet and, wherever possible, destroy enemy shipping. Along the Rio Grande he also created more suspicion by attempting to establish a buffer zone through closer commercial ties with the people. He even suggested several colonization plans for the area but each one met an ignominious fate in Congress, thanks to the Houston opposition. But most important to Lamar were the settlements on the Upper Rio Grande. Here was, he believed, the area for immediate expansion, the path of glory, the course of empire. When Congress refused his request for an expedition to march on Santa Fe, he injudiciously took it upon himself in June, 1841, to finance merchants and soldiers who would help him fulfill his foremost dreams.

Unfortunately the venture was a dismal failure for all concerned, a fiasco filled with brutality and death. Its strategy was ill-conceived and naive, its purpose visionary; yet the results of this disastrous action were far-reaching, principally in regard to annexation. For once again Texans, with their vision no longer impaired by promises of an easy military victory, by grandiose dreams of empire, began to realize the harsh realities of maintaining an independent republic. Financial problems—indebtedness, inflation, tariff duties—were unbelievably complex and, at times, seemed insurmountable. For the moment the Indians appeared to be subdued and the frontier areas relatively safe, but now a much more dangerous menace had arisen. Because of Lamar's blundering militancy Mexico was preparing an invasion force which would endanger once more the very existence of Texas. And after the barbarous treatment accorded the prisoners of the Santa Fe expedition, Texans—and many Americans too—felt that, since no people should be subject to such dire consequences, annexation would offer the easiest and most sensible solution.

Equally significant to this line of reasoning were diplomatic pressures exerted by the Lamar Administration. In 1839-1840 Henderson and James Hamilton, the Republic's representatives in Europe, had succeeded in wringing a recognition of independence as well as commercial treaties from England, France, and the Netherlands. As far as financial aid, these agreements were insignificant; yet, merely by the fact that Texas was receiving and accepting foreign assistance led to rumors of all shapes and sizes. What were the British planning for Texas? Were they seriously attempting to re-establish a new empire in the American West? More and more the answers to such questions, embellished by the imagination of each talebearer, began to alarm some Americans, especially Southerners. And when Lamar left office on December 13, 1841, such suspicions had contributed to reawakening the latent thoughts on annexation.

Succeeding him as President was an old adversary, Sam Houston, who—as Lamar had done for the past three years—continued the administrative game of "Fruit Basket Turnover." One by one "Old Sam" negated or reversed the major programs of Lamar. Of course, a friendly policy towards the Indians replaced search and destroy tactics; a stress on economy and frugality, to the point of being painfully parsimonious, was quite different from the heavy spending allowed in promoting an empire; and instead of a steadfast governmental stand for an independent republic, a strong movement for annexation evolved.

Of all the issues which would confront this Houston Administration, annexation was by far the most important, holding sway over the Texas political leaders, dominating their thoughts while hypnotizing the public. And even though this delicate and intricate diplomatic question was fraught with numerous pitfalls, any one of which might have wrecked negotiations, Houston was at his best, inscrutable and unpredictable, at times magnificently Machiavellian. Like a master chess player he developed his plan of attack, not through obvious or patterned moves which could easily be countered but through complex and oftentimes mystifying procedures. When venturing into an unexplored area, he used his wits and judgment and long experience to guide him; when past rules did not apply, he invented new ones; and no matter how difficult the problem he applied himself to whatever it required and demanded.

First of all Houston laid a firm foundation for his program by selecting good men, whereupon painstakingly and sagaciously he worked to produce the desired results. After much forethought he chose Dr. Anson Jones, an experienced and trusted friend, as secretary of state, James Reily as minister to Washington, and Ashbel Smith as minister to England and France. Then on January 26, 1842, he instructed Reily through Jones to "be discreet and suave" in mentioning the idea of annexation. At all times he should, as the Texas minister, appear noncommittal, yet "whisper to the United States that the door was no longer locked."

The approach was proper, the timing excellent, as the events of the next twelve months would verify. For what could arouse more sympathy than a people under invasion and attack? In March and again in September a Mexican army marched into Texas, on both occasions capturing San Antonio. Since Houston was on "an economy kick," the Republic had no regular army for defense, only enraged and fearsome volunteer militia who wanted to inflict a horrible punishment on their tormentors. In fact, upon repelling the second Mexican invasion, General Alexander Somervell with approximately 700 men advanced to the Rio Grande and on December 8 captured Laredo. After several weeks of confusion and indecision he retired with part of his force while some 500 Texans, more chauvinistic and vindictive, marched across the river to Mier. On Christmas Day they encountered General Pedro de Ampudia with an army of 2,000 men who killed or captured most of them after a day-long, hard-fought battle. Of the survivors one out of ten was forced to draw a fatal, death-dealing black bean, while the rest rotted for months in a filthy prison.

So with examples of Mexican brutality and inhumanity before them, with Texans (although obviously unprepared) clamoring for war to redress grievances, with agents of the Republic raising funds and enlisting bellicose "emigrants" at huge rallies in Philadelphia and New York, the United States became gravely concerned. After all, there was some question whether Texas could maintain its independence—much less withstand another Mexican attack—especially if the widespread rumors were true that British loans had financed the 1842 invasions. Increasingly important also were economic considerations; already Northern businessmen were beginning to enjoy substantial profits from Texas trade as the population increased and transportation improved. But what caused the greatest anxiety and alarm were British negotiations with the Republic. Much like the Spanish in the seventeenth and eighteenth centuries, Americans usually reinvigorated their diplomacy when a Europeon power threatened their interests.

No one understood the American character or for that matter knew mass public psychology better than Sam Houston—and in 1843 he proved it. To Charles Elliot, the British chargé d'affaires, he was exceedingly cordial and friendly, so much so that by June, 1843, "common talk" reported him to be "completely under British influence." Nor did he try to hide his displeasure with American foreign policy, its apathetic rather condescending attitude towards his past efforts, for on several occasions he pointedly announced that, with British help, independence was "all that Texas requires," not annexation. To give more substance to this story of disenchantment he allowed rumors to go unchallenged that he had turned abolitionist, that anti-slave English merchants were preparing to loan the Republic huge sums of money, and that he had agreed with Elliot, as the *Telegraph and Texas Register* related, to abolish slavery if the British would force Mexico to sign an armistice. And no matter that he was receiving widespread criticism and public censure for thwarting the popular will through "secret" negotiations, he continued to maintain this difficult and, for the moment, unrewarding pose.

Houston would soon escape further villification, however, as his calculations began to materialize and events vindicated his strategy. Yet his foreign policy might well have failed without the support of the President of the United States. A staunch States' Righter from Virginia and an ardent admirer of John C. Calhoun, President John Tyler dreamed of easing, if not eliminating, many of the difficulties which had plagued both nations for the past few years. To him only one solution was feasible— annexation. As early as April, 1841, he had wanted such a union but with the possibility of Senate ratification unlikely he had bided his time. But as rumors of Anglo-Texian rapport persisted and then multiplied throughout the United States, he decided to press his advantage. In September he instructed Secretary of State Abel P. Upshur to inform the Texas delegation of his desires; in October he proposed treaty negotiations; and in December he asked Congress to help secure peace between Mexico and Texas. He even enlisted former President Andrew Jackson in his cause by getting him to write a "pressure letter" to Sam Houston. In fact, the continuing threat of Great Britain proved to be a windfall to his plans, an effective argument against his enemies, an excuse for action. During January and February, 1844, therefore, he pushed negotiations, hoping that Upshur would promptly conclude a treaty.

At the same time Houston was being, as Llerena Friend put it, "more coy than forward"—and for good reason. Since every annexation effort had failed in the last seven years, he had to anticipate all possibilities in order to protect himself and his people. Before agreeing to preliminary talks for formal annexation (which the United States Senate might reject), he instructed the Texas commissioners to demand certain safeguards. Because such meetings would undoubtedly provoke Mexico, possibly to the point of another invasion, he wanted definite guarantees from Tyler that the United States army and navy would be ordered to defend the Republic throughout the negotiations. Then, and only then, would he consider annexation. In turn, he cultivated the British and French who desired to block any proposed union. Quite often he encouraged them by purposely making negative statements about American diplomacy or by asserting that, in connection with the United States, Texans must never "submit to unreasonable and unjust sacrifices." As an alternative to President Tyler's proposals he indicated that, if England and France would force Mexico to recognize Texas independence, he would be most favorably inclined. Either way, Houston was not going to lose; by playing one nation off against the other, he was solidifying his position.

Despite Houston's inscrutable strategy, the Texas commissioners in Washington, J. Pinckney Henderson and Isaac Van Zandt, were rapidly concluding a satisfactory agreement with the United States when an unfortunate accident disrupted all diplomatic maneuvering. Other than a temporary delay, the result effect was merely a change in personnel, not in attitude. What happened was that Secretary of State Upshur, who had been vigorously pushing for annexation, accepted a weekend invitation by the United States Navy to observe the experimental and supposedly revolutionary guns on the sloop of war *Princeton*. On February 28, 1844, one of the turrets suddenly blew up, killing him and several other prominent officials. For almost a month thereafter negotiations ceased until John C. Calhoun, the new Secretary of State, oriented hmself. By the end of March, however, he had taken up with renewed vigor where his predecessor had left off. And on April 12 Henderson and Van Zandt happily signed a treaty of annexation.

But unfortunately circumstances doomed this agreement from the beginning. The timing was poor, psychological effects different from what the signers had expected. With Calhoun as Secretary of State the annexation question now smacked of sectionalism, of Southern intrigue, of "slavocracy," and therefore took on national importance. Once again abolitionists pressured the nation, warning the people against Southerners who were conspiring to turn western lands into slave brothels, who were at that moment surreptitiously trying to obscure the real issue by appealing to American pride and patriotism through expansionism. And although Houston cajoled and warned the United States Senate that annexation was "now or never," that Texas would turn hereafter to England and France, his comments were no longer effective. It was an election year; politicians were uneasy; no one could gauge or predict the public temper accurately. So at first Congress temporized until President Tyler forced the issue. On June 10, 1844, the Senators defeated the treaty 35 to 16.

Yet annexation was by no means a dead issue. If anything, success appeared more likely in the next few months than ever before; such a union, shrewd political observers predicted, was only a matter of time. On June 12 for instance, just two days after the Senate rejection and prior to legislative adjournment, President Tyler sent documents regarding Texas to the House of Representatives. Under this pretext he proposed annexation by an act of Congress, thereby placing the question before the public once again. In turn, both major parties addressed themselves to the specific issue, confident that the voters in November would vindicate their stands in the Presidential election. For Henry Clay and the Whigs, equivocation was in order. He was not necessarily for annexation, he asserted, unless war with Mexico could be averted and all sections of the nation appeased. For James K. Polk and the Democrats, however, the emphasis was on Manifest Destiny, for they adopted a platform which endorsed "the reoccupation of Oregon and the reannexation of Texas at the earliest practicable period." Quickly across the land there resounded the catchy campaign slogans of "Fifty-four-forty or fight" and the "Annexation of Texas." And even though the vote was extremely close, the Democrats won. Polk believed that he had received a clear mandate for expansionism and glory.

For his four years in office the new President-elect had definite goals in mind such as lowering the tariff, establishing a new Sub-Treasury system, and acquiring California. But John Tyler would rob him of one ambition—the annexation of Texas. In his annual message to Congress on December 4, 1844, the President once more opened the question by urging the legislators to act promptly. No Americans would ever forget the heroic stand of Texans at the Alamo, the barbarous massacre at Goliad, the senseless inhumanities of the Santa Fe and Mier expeditions, he asserted, or permit any nation guilty of such atrocities to rule over former Americans. Nor could they ever allow a foreign power to block their way to the Pacific, to deny them their Manifest Destiny. If the congressmen had any doubts regarding these statements, they needed to look no further than the recent elections. The people had spoken unmistakably. So the answer, he concluded, was quite simple—a joint act of Congress.

Surprisingly the legislators responded rather quickly to Tyler's request. In less than two months they proposed and amended a number of bills until a satisfactory product emerged. At length they agreed that Texas would be admitted into the Union if its people consented to such action by January 1, 1846. As a state among equals it would retain all public lands (and debts too), be guaranteed a republican form of government, and allowed to form four other states from its territory, none of which would be slave if above the 36°30' line of the Missouri Compromise. Concerning state boundaries nothing was done for the moment; the problem was too complex, the time too short. The United States promised, however, to make the proper adjustments at a later date. And if perchance some complication arose as to the method of annexation, the President could negotiate, if he so chose, along any lines that both nations approved.

On March 3, 1845, a few hours before leaving office, President Tyler signed the bill affecting Texas. Then the struggle among world diplomats began; for now those who had opposed this union pooled their resources for one last desperate fight to block it. Charles Elliot, the British chargé d'affaires and close friend to Houston, urged his government to act decisively—and at once—in forcing Mexico to guarantee Texas independence. "Several leading men in the country," he announced, would "declare themselves against annexation," if they could do so "without mischief to their popularity." What they were looking for, he explained, was a choice, a way out, or even just an excuse. On these assumptions the British and French governments applied intense pressure to Mexican officials in behalf of Texas independence. In turn, Elliot persuaded President Anson Jones, who had succeeded Houston in September, 1844, to approve preliminary peace terms which Texas might be willing to consider. The overall idea was that, if Mexico guaranteed independence, the Republic would agree to reject all future annexation offers, that it would hereafter steer an independent course. But regardless of the outcome of these negotiations, a ninety-day moratorium would go into effect to allow adequate time for discussion.

Undoubtedly Elliot believed President Jones to be one of those prominent men who was against annexation, and in large measure he was right.

For even though Jones had renounced the Houston Administration in September, 1844, for attempting to conclude commercial agreements with England and France, he had done so out of a desire for political self-preservation, out of a fear that such alliances "would either defeat annexation altogether, or lead to a war between Europe and America." Actually Jones was much like Houston in that he wanted alternatives which would be concrete proposals rather than alluring promises. So he worked, as he later recorded, "for annexation and independence at the same time." He chose the middle ground, or so he claimed, yet most of his diplomatic appointees were anti-American and his actions definitely seemed to favor British strategy. After all, he was delaying a decision on annexation for at least nniety days while President Polk was explicitly urging speed.

If Anson Jones appeared to be against annexation, he was not alone; many prominent Texas leaders either secretly or openly opposed it. Secretary of State Ashbel Smith and Attorney General Ebenezer Allen were markedly hostile as were all the cabinet members except Secretary of the Treasury William Ochiltree; James Reily, minister to Washington, wrote: "We must either have annexation or peace before we can prosper and Peace we could with independent action have at once"; while Sam Houston, it was rumored, wanted to reject the present treaty and have Texans draw up a more favorable one.

But among the populace there was no question; annexation must be approved. On April 29, 1845, Andrew Jackson Donelson, the new American minister to Texas, immediately sensed the public temper upon arriving at Galveston; however, he took no chances. To President Jones he publicly pledged that the United States would shower innumerable benefits upon Texas—river and harbor improvements, lighthouses for coastal commerce, forts and soldiers for frontier defense, as well as "employment, wealth, and prosperity." A month later Elliot also reached Galveston after having forced the Mexican government to guarantee Texas independence. But he was not happy at the prospects. On every hand citizens were holding mass meetings and county conventions, demanding immediate action on annexation. Increasingly anti-British and suspicious of any Mexican overture, they vented their frustrations on Anson Jones, criticizing his dilatory tactics and his open "collusion" with England. Even after he called for a state constitutional convention to meet in Austin on July 4, they were unappeased. After all, he was now doing what was politically expedient, what they had forced him to do.

As soon as the machinery was set in motion for statehood, however, the public furor gradually subsided and annexation became a matter of public record. On June 16 at Washington-on-the-Brazos, President Jones convened Congress, whereupon he submitted the offers from both the United States and Mexico. Unanimously the legislators accepted annexation. Then on July 4 delegates met in Austin to consider the American proposal and with only one dissenting vote agreed to join the Union. For the next two months they drew up a state constitution which was submitted to the people on October 13 and quickly ratified. And finally on December 29, 1845, with Texans having fulfilled all requirements of a "republican form of government," President Polk signed the bill which admitted Texas into the Union. All that remained now was the formality of a ceremony.

It was noon on February 19, 1846, when President Anson Jones mounted the flag-draped platform in front of Representative Hall in Austin. Since Texans had rejected him as a leader in the new state, he had come to perform one final duty to the Republic, to lend decorum and dignity to this joyous occasion. He had prepared a short speech, actually just a few minutes in length. But in these last moments as President, he somehow captured the feeling and emotion of everyone about him—and suddenly a hush fell over the crowd. "The lone star of Texas which ten years since arose amid clouds over fields of carnage, and obscurely shone for a while, has culminated," he eloquently announced, "and, following an inscrutable destiny, has passed on and become fixed forever in that glorious constellation . . . the American Union. . . . The final act in this great drama is now performed," he concluded. "The Republic of Texas is no more." Then quickly in the silence that followed he stepped forward and lowered the Texas flag. The cannon boomed, breaking the spell he had woven, and the crowd began to cheer. Texas had at last become a state among equals.

The Confederate States
of America

1861 - 1865

Sam Houston's Moment of Decision -- March 16, 1861

Texas Joins the Confederacy

By

HAROLD B. SIMPSON

Ye men of valor gather round the banner of the right,
Texas and fair Louisiana join us in the fight;
Davis, our loved President, and Stephens, statesman rare,
Now rally round the Bonnie Blue Flag that bears a single star.
                                                    —Harry Macarthy

Texas was annexed to the United States as the twenty-eighth star in the Federal constellation on December 29, 1845, and she was the seventh state to withdraw from the Federal Union during the Confederate era of the 1860's. The first marriage between the former republic and the United States was a brief one, but an extremely profitable one for the Lone Star State. Texas was annexed under extremely favorable terms. She was the only state to join the Federal Union that was permitted to retain her public lands and the only state that was given the opportunity to sub-divide herself if she so chose. Economic expansion and population explosion marked the decade and a half that Texas sent representatives to Washington prior to the Civil War.

This period of "early statehood" was one of tremendous prosperity, a period of great growth and steady progress that was unmatched by any other state for a like period of time. From fewer than 400,000 head of cattle in 1846, Texas could count almost 4,000,000 head by 1860. Cotton production jumped from fewer than 40,000 bales in 1848 to over 420,000 bales twelve years later. Other crops showed similar increases. However, even more significant than the growth in agriculture was the great attraction that Texas held for both the American and the foreign immigrant. At the time of annexation, the total population of the state was estimated at between 125,000 and 150,000. By 1850 the number had increased to 212,000—and by 1860 the total population figure had soared to over 600,000. Thus Texas, with her great agricultural wealth and substantial population, was worthy of the courtship tendered her by the states of the "Old South" and the Confederate government at Montgomery.

It was inevitable that the Lone Star State would embrace a Southern Confederacy when and if one was established. The bulk of the state's population in 1860 was composed of first generation Southerners from

Mississippi, Tennessee, Alabama, and Arkansas. Most of her influential statesmen, newspaper editors, and large landowners were pro-slavery or states' rights advocates. Her greatest cash crop was cotton, and her greatest single investment was in the 183,000 slaves working in the cane and cotton fields. Financially, morally, and politically Texas was geared to a cotton-slave economy.

One man and really only one man stood between Texas and secession. His stature was great, both physically and politically. He had commanded the Texian army in its greatest hour—San Jacinto on April 21, 1836. He had served the Republic of Texas twice as its president and then had served the state of Texas as United States Senator. Sam Houston, protege of Andrew Jackson, had been instrumental in bringing Texas into the Union and then had guided her national destiny from his seat in the Senate. He was most reluctant to see "his" state slip back out of the Union. General Houston was an ardent champion of the Federal Constitution and of the obligations and the responsibilities that the various states owed to this holy compact. But Sam Houston, even with his great personal prestige, his logical reasoning, his gift of oratory, and his position as the chief executive of the state, was swept aside by the wave of secession that engulfed the state in 1860 and early 1861.

Houston had been elected governor of Texas in 1859 in one of the bitterest gubernatorial contests staged in the Lone Star State. His opponent in 1859, incumbent Hardin R. Runnels, had defeated the General in the race for governor two years before and thus could boast that he had been the only man ever to defeat Sam Houston in a political election. In 1857, Houston had conducted a lack-lustre campaign representing the disorganized remnants of the Whig and the Know-Nothing element in Texas against the regular Democratic organization. But in 1859 it was a far different story. In the intervening years the leaders of the regular Democratic Party had become aggressively and openly secessionist minded and had talked of re-opening the slave trade and of annexing Cuba and Mexico. This contemplated action and grandiose talk of the Democrats alienated the large uncommitted conservative Texas vote, and the small but stalwart pro-Union group in the state who organized behind Houston. Running as an "Independent National Democrat," the old Warrior stumped the state in a vigorous (and vitriolic) campaign for the "Constitution and the Union." Ably assisted by such avowed Unionists as Elisha M. Pease, David Burnet, J. W. Throckmorton, B. H. Epperson, and A. J. Hamilton—and loud in his denunciation of the frontier and financial policies of Runnels—Houston swept to victory by a comfortable margin.

Sam Houston was to know little peace during his fourteen months in the executive mansion. When he took the oath of office as the seventh elected governor of Texas on December 21, 1859, the national political situation was rapidly drifting toward open hostility between the North and the South. Bleeding Kansas, where "Beecher's Bibles" faced Mississippi Rifles, was still wracked by dissension, distrust, and disunion. John Brown's raid on Harpers Ferry, Virginia, in October, 1859, had further incensed an already alarmed South, while Brown's prosecution and subsequent hanging was loudly denounced in the North. Convenient interpretations and irregular actions associated with the Compromise of 1850, The Kansas-Nebraska Act, and the Dred Scott Decision further widened the schism between the two sections of the country. The tenseness of the situation that existed at the national level filtered down into the various states as the specter of "irrepressible conflict" haunted the halls of Congress, and an air of foreboding doom settled over the country.

The full impact of this widespread feeling of uneasiness and sectional tension hit Texas in 1860. The crime rate increased alarmingly as law enforcement was generally relaxed throughout the state. To compound the internal unrest, Juan Cortina, the self-styled "Mexican Robin Hood," was active on both sides of the Rio Grande and the Apaches and Comanches staged daring raids along the western frontier. Near hysteria gripped the state as incendiary fires were reported in various sections of North Texas, supposedly set by slaves or meddling abolitionists. Dallas was partially destroyed by a $300,000 blaze, and other major fires occurred simultaneously at Denton, Gainesville, Waxahachie, and Corsicana. Caches of arms and quantities of poison were reportedly found in the hands of Negroes, and rumors of organized slave uprisings and assassinations quickly spread throughout the state. Most of these reports later proved to be grossly exaggerated or to be entirely unfounded, but not before several hangings had taken place. In Dallas three Negroes were hanged for engaging "in a conspiracy" and Fort Worth, not to be outdone by its rival North Texas community, hanged three white men (reported to be abolitionists) for "tampering with slaves." In other parts of the state individual hangings, lynchings, and banishments took place. Vigilante committees and local military committees bearing audacious names were formed to combat the anxiety and the fears that seemed to paralyze the population.

The mass hysteria which appeared to grip the state in mid-1860 was fanned, if indeed it was not perpetrated, by a para-military, semi-secret group known as the Knights of the Golden Circle. With headquarters at San Antonio, the "Knights" established lodges or "castles" in many of the larger towns of Texas, including Austin, Brenham, Chappell Hill, Houston, Navasota, and Waco. Carrying on its activities both clandestinely and openly, the organization aggressively pursued its reported aims to re-open the African slave trade, extend slavery into the territories, and to include northern Mexico in the "slave empire." The organization was thought to have numbered close to 8,000. The Knights were active in politics, and there is evidence they controlled the official action of the Democratic Party in the state. Many of the leading secessionists in Texas were directly or indirectly affiliated with the activities and aims of this group. The seedbed of secession in Texas was nurtured to maturity by the Knights of the Golden Circle.

Despite the crusading efforts of Governor Houston and his Unionist friends, Texas politically as well as emotionally swung rapidly toward secession as 1860 drew to a close. To help set the stage for the secession showdown, which occurred during the winter of 1860-61, the State Legislature had declared sides a few days before Houston's inauguration by selecting Louis T. Wigfall to take the General's place in the United States Senate. Wigfall, a bombastic South Carolinian who had emigrated to Texas in the late 1840's, was a bitter opponent of Sam Houston and a leading advocate for the re-opening of the African slave trade and for secession. The anti-Union sentiment of the Democratic Party in Texas was further emphasized at the Democratic state convention held at Galveston in April, 1860. The states' rights leaders, who were in full control of the convention, proclaimed the legal right of secession and hinted that the election of a "Black Republican" as president would be grounds for terminating the Union. To cement its decision for secession, the state convention nominated five staunch supporters of slavery to attend the Democratic national convention in Charleston, South Carolina—Hardin Runnels, Francis Lubbock, Guy Bryan, Richard Hubbard, and Tom Ochiltree. The five Texans helped to select John C. Breckinridge of Kentucky as the standard bearer for the Southern faction of the Democratic Party in the national election of 1860.

Although not one popular vote was counted for Abraham Lincoln in the deep South, the Illinois Republican garnered enough electoral votes from the heavily populated Northen states to win the election. The split of the Democratic Party into a northern and a southern faction and the presence of the Constitutional Union Party in the 1860 election, scattered the opposition effectively to insure the Republican victory. Although Lincoln, a Southerner by birth, was opposed to the spread of slavery into the territories, he had promised the South that he would not interfere with their "peculiar institution" where it already existed. Regardless of the president-elect's declaration, the South feared the worst, and the Republican victory was the signal for the cotton states to start their exodus from the Union.

In Texas, Lincoln's victory at the polls noticeably increased the anti-Union sentiment in the state and drove most of the fence-sitters and many of the conservatives into the secessionist camp. Governor Houston and the Unionists, realizing the tide of disunion was rising, endeavored to stay the tide by recommending caution and careful consideration of the consequences that secession was bound to bring. It was Houston's firm belief that the election of Lincoln, although he deplored it, was not justification enough for dissolving the Union. He believed that the grievances of the South could and would be satisfied by working arrangements within the framework of the Constitution. General Houston prophesied that Lincoln would not let the Southern states exit in peace, that the "Railsplitter" would fight to hold the nation together, and thus secession would mean civil war. The "Hero of San Jacinto" cautioned that in an armed conflict the South would be no match for the North with its extensive resources of manpower, materiel, and wealth and that war would bring only destruction and bankruptcy to Texas and the South. Unfortunately for the South, Houston's prophecy proved to be correct on all counts.

Governor Houston used every device and delaying tactic possible to forestall anti-Union action by the powerful secessionist element in the state. On November 28, 1860, the old soldier made his first move. He took advantage of a state law passed in 1858 during the Kansas crisis. According to this statute the governor was authorized to call for the election of seven delegates to meet in convention with representatives of the other Southern states when such a meeting became necessary "to preserve the equal rights of such States in the Union." Houston sent a copy of the Texas statute to the governors of the Southern states, recommending that a congress of conciliation be held at Austin to consider concerted action in the light of Lincoln's election. By this move Houston hoped to satisfy the Texas radicals and thwart any plans that they might have for unilateral action. Houston's recommendation, however, fell on deaf ears—not one governor even acknowledged receipt of the invitation.

According to John S. "Rip" Ford, Texas Ranger and Mexican War hero, the Governor tried yet another subterfuge to delay action by the state secessionists. Ford reported that Governor Houston approached Supreme Court Judges R. T. Wheeler and J. H. Bell and requested that they prepare for him a constitutional rebuttal to the doctrine of secession. The Governor's idea was to issue the circular to stem the agitation for withdrawal from the Union. If such a request was made by the Governor, it was not acted upon by the judges, or at least a copy of such a circular, if such did exist, has not survived.

Sam Houston was denounced throughout the South for his pro-Union stand and for his efforts to put the lid on the anti-Union movement in the Lone Star State. Senator Wigfall, to whom Houston in contempt referred to as "Senator Wiggletail," stated before a secessionist gathering in Virginia that the Governor of Texas "ought to be tarred and feathered and driven from the state." Senator Alfred Iverson of Georgia, another bitter foe of Houston's, went so far as to hint at the General's assassination when he said that "some Texas Brutus may arise to rid his country of this hoary-headed traitor." Although constantly badgered and ridiculed by the secessionist element, the Texas giant gave ground begrudgingly. Houston was a man of principle, and he believed in the sanctity of the Federal Constitution.

The Governor, however, was finally forced to take some action in regard to the future role of the state. He was deluged daily with petitions, editorials, and letters from every quarter, most of which requested that he call a special session of the Legislature to consider the question of secession. The harried old hero finally agreed to call the special session, but only after a sizeable body of prominent citizens, acting in concert, forced his hand.

On December 3, 1860, a group of state officials gathered in Attorney General George M. Flournoy's office to draw up a plan for circumventing the Governor. This group, led by Flournoy, W. S. Oldham, John Marshall, W. P. Rogers, John S. Ford, and Associate Justice Oran M. Roberts of the State Supreme Court, drew up a petition calling for the election of delegates to meet at Austin on January 28, 1861, for the purpose of deciding the future of Texas. The petition listed the following reasons for calling the convention: (1) the election of a sectional president, (2) the imminent danger to Southern rights, (3) the Governor's refusal to convene the Legislature, (4) the sovereign will of the people could best be expressed by a convention, (5) the Governor or the Legislature could not call a convention as only the people had the right to do so, and (6) there was not enough time before the inauguration of Lincoln for the Legislature to act.

Within a matter of days the petition was signed by some sixty leading Texas secessionists, including legislators, jurists, businessmen, newspaper editors and professional men. The petition was subsequently published in the Austin *State-Gazette*. Thus the issue was joined—the gauntlet of secession was tossed at Houston. He had to act now or face a possible civil war in Texas. Caught between two fires, the Governor chose to deal with the Legislature. He issued a call on December 17, 1860, for an extra session of the Legislature to meet on January 21—one week before the scheduled meeting of the Convention. It was Houston's hope that the Legislature, the "legally" elected body representing the people, would outlaw the Convention and forestall the movement to take Texas out of the Union.

The interval between the publication of the petition and the meeting of the Convention was marked by stump speaking, political pressuring, and big barbecues. The leaders on both sides canvassed the state, pleading their causes. Governor Houston's initial target was the Galveston area, the largest population center of pre-war Texas and one of the centers of secessionist power. The Governor was warned by his friends to avoid speaking in the port city. He had been denied use of the best hall in town, and it was rumored that an attempt might be made on his life. Relishing the challenge, the General spoke from the balcony of the Tremont House to a throng that packed the street. Greeted by catcalls and hisses as he started to speak, the old Hero of San Jacinto soon had the audience on his side and on numerous occasions vigorous handclapping punctuated his oration. Thomas North, a Northerner who lived in Texas during the war, was a spectator at Houston's Galveston speech and left a vivid picture of how the Governor looked in the autumn of his career espousing a cause that he held dear.

> There he stood, an old man of seventy [67] years, on the balconey [sic] ten feet above the heads of the thousands assembled to hear him, where every eye could scan his magnificient [sic] form, six feet three inches high, straight as an arrow, with deep set and penetrating eyes, looking out from under heavy and thundering eyebrows, a high open forehead, with something of the infinite intellectual shadowed there, crowned with thin white locks, partly erect, seeming to give capillary condition to the electric fluid used by his massive brain, and a voice of the deep basso tone, which shook and commanded the soul of the hearer. Adding to all this a powerful manner, made up of deliberation, self-possession and restrained majesty of action, leaving the hearer impressed with the feeling that more of his power was hidden than revealed. Thus appeared Sam Houston on this grand occasion, equal and superior to it, as he always was to every other. He paralyzed the mobocrat by his personal presence, and it was morally impossible for him to be mobbed in Texas.

After cautioning his listeners about the pitfalls associated with secession and then extolling the numerous benefits bestowed by the Federal Constitution, the General closed his speech with a vibrant climax that left little doubt of how highly he regarded the Lone Star State.

> Whatever course my State shall determine to pursue my faith in State Supremacy and State rights will carry my sympathies with her. And, as Henry Clay, my political opponent on annexation said, when asked why he allowed his son to go into the Mexican War, "My country, right or wrong," so I say, my State, right or wrong.

Houston followed his Galveston speech with major speeches at Houston and at Waco. The city of Houston, another anti-Union stronghold, was hostile to its chief executive. The Bayou City crowds interrupted his fervent pleas for the Union repeatedly with shouts of "Three Cheers for Toombs," "Three Cheers for Yancey," "Three Cheers for South Carolina," and the most stinging shout of all—"Three Cheers for Wigfall!" The Governor spoke at Waco on New Year's Day, 1861, and for the first time publicly stated that if Texas did leave the Union—if the people did demand secession by popular vote—the state should revert to its former independent status of a republic rather than join in the Southern conspiracy. This new approach by the Governor so incensed the secessionist leaders of McLennan County that the Unionists in Waco urged Houston to cross the Brazos before nightfall and leave the area. The Governor refused to be intimidated, but his sleep was interrupted that night by the explosion of a keg of gunpowder behind his hotel. On the following day Sam Houston leisurely left town.

Regardless of the herculean efforts extended by Houston, Throckmorton, Pease, Davis, Hamilton, and the other prominent Unionists, the wave of secession engulfed the state. Even before the petition calling for a convention had been published several counties had taken the initiative to select delegates to a general state convention to consider the matter of separation from the Union. Other counties held their elections before the date specified by the petition (January 8, 1861). The aggressive leaders of secession carried everything before them after the announcement of the Republican victory.

The special session of the Eighth Legislature called by Houston, convened as planned on January 21, 1861. Houston's message on this occasion is considered to be one of the General's outstanding state papers. Most of his address was concerned with the internal affairs of Texas, and he outlined enough work to keep the legislators busy for at least a year. No doubt this was part of Houston's strategy: to concentrate on the many internal problems that plagued Texas to take attention away from the major problem of the moment—Federal-State relations. However, the

Governor did dwell at some length upon the question of the day: "The peculiar attitude of our relations with the Federal government. . . ." Houston expressed regret that they were seeing "the proud structure of government, built by our fathers . . . tottering in ruins," but cautioned his fellow Texans that the "election of the Black Republican candidate," while regrettable was "no cause for the . . . immediate secession of Texas." The Governor, falling back on the approach that he had used from the beginning toward secession, counseled delay and hoped that "one rash act" would not blur Texas' glorious page in history.

At no time in his speech did Governor Houston refer directly to the Convention that was to convene on January 28, even though that was the issue paramount in the minds of most Texans at the moment. The Legislature, however, made up for the governor's slight by extending the red carpet treatment to the convention delegates. Several of the delegates were invited to sit within the bar of the Senate and the House when they arrived in Austin. The Legislature not only voted to recognize the authority of the convention (over Houston's veto) but for purposes of prestige also voted to allow the convention to meet in the hall of the House of Representatives after two o'clock each day. To provide for the comforts of the convention delegates, fuel, ink, and stationery were placed at their disposal. The Legislators also passed a resolution providing the delegates with *per diem* and giving them a mileage allowance to and from Austin. Only in one instance did the Legislature attempt to qualify the action of the convention: if an ordinance of secession was adopted it would have to be submitted to a vote of the electorate to be effective.

The Secession Convention convened on schedule at two o'clock on the afternoon of Monday, January 28, 1861. It met in the hall of the House of Representatives with 170 delegates present. Seven more delegates reported on January 30, bringing the total number of delegates attending to 177. John D. Stell of Leon County was appointed president *pro tempore* to preside over the election of officers. Oran M. Roberts was elected president of the convention; R. T. Brownrigg, secretary; W. D. School-field, first assistant secretary; and R. H. Lundy, second assistant secretary. Roberts engaged in a bit of heroics when, taking the president's chair, he turned to the delegates and exclaimed: "I bow to the sovereignty of the people of my state!" Thus the convention commenced in dramatic style!

With the details of organization out of the way, the balance of the first day's meeting was spent in debating the question of whether or not the ordinance of secession (when it was effected) should be submitted to a vote of the people. Earlier the Legislature had declared that such an ordinance must be ratified by the electorate to be binding. A test of authority between the two bodies was averted when the convention voted 140 to 28 to comply with the Legislature's action.

On the second day of meeting (January 29) the direct issue before the convention came up. John A. Wharton of Brazoria County introduced a resolution "that the state of Texas should separately secede from the Federal Union." Wharton's resolution was adopted by a vote of 157 to 8. Following the vote on the secession resolution, several other actions took place, the most important one being the selection of a Committee on Federal Relations. It was the purpose of this committee to draw up an Ordinance of Secession. Twenty of the most ardent secessionists were appointed to the committee, including W. B. Ochiltree, George Flournoy, John A. Wharton, Peter Gray, Joseph Hogg, F. S. Stockdale, John Gregg, T. J. Chambers, and Richard Coke. Most of the men serving on this keystone committee rose to high civil or military rank during the war.

Desiring to act in harmony with both the Governor and the Legislature and in order to solicit their support (particularly Governor Houston's), two liaison committees of five men each were appointed on January 29 by the convention. A committee headed by John H. Reagan and composed of P. W. Gray, John O. Stell, Thomas J. Devine, and W. P. Rogers was selected to wait upon the Governor. According to Reagan, the Governor received the committee (on January 30) with "due respect, expressed his thanks for this action of the convention, and assured [them] that he would communicate his views in writing on tomorrow [January 31]. . . ." In communicating his views to the convention, Governor Houston stated that

> whatever will conduce to the welfare of our people will have my warmest and most fervent wishes, and when the voice of the people of Texas has been declared through the ballot box, no citizen will be more ready to yield obedience to its will or risk his all in its defense than myself. . . .

He further stated that he would ". . . act in harmony with the convention in securing an expression of the popular will in the matter touching on Federal relations and that [he] would cheerfully confer with any committee appointed for the purpose." Beyond these statements the Governor did not commit himself.

During the meetings of the convention held on January 30 and 31, the main order of business was the debate on the Ordinance of Secession placed before the convention by the Committee on Federal Relations. After meeting in several secret sessions, during which time many proposed amendments were considered, the Ordinance as originally reported out of committee on January 30 was adopted. The Texas Ordinance of Secession read as follows:

> Section 1. Whereas, the Federal Government has failed to accomplish the purposes of the compact of union between these states in giving protection either to the persons of our people upon an exposed frontier or to the property of our citizens; and whereas the action of the Northern states of the union, and the recent development in Federal affairs, make it evident that the power of the Federal government is sought to be made a weapon with which to strike down the interests and prosperity of the Southern people, instead of permitting it to be as it was intended, our shield against outrage and aggression.

> Therefore, we the people of the state of Texas in convention do declare and ordain, that the ordinance adopted by our convention of delegates on the 4th day of July, A. D. 1845, and afterwards ratified by us, under which the Republic of Texas was admitted into the Union with other states and became a party to the compact styled "The Constitution of the United States of America" be and is hereby repealed and annulled; that all the powers that by said compact were delegated by Texas to the Federal government are revoked and resumed; that Texas is of right absolved from all restraints and obligations incurred by said compact and is a separate sovereign state.

> Section 2. This ordinance shall be submitted to the people of Texas for ratification or rejection by the qualified voters on the 23rd day of February, A. D. 1861, and unless rejected by a majority of the votes cast shall take effect and be in force on and after the 2nd day of March, A. D. 1861.

On the evening of January 31, it was resolved that the third reading and the vote on the Ordinance would take place the following day. It was further resolved that no discussion would take place when the vote was taken. Two dramatic incidents were to violate the "no discussion resolution."

On February 1, 1861, in the hall of the House of Representatives at Austin unfolded one of the most dramatic moments in Texas history. On this day, at a few minutes past twelve o'clock noon, Texas would vote herself out of the Federal Union. The action taken on this day would involve the state in one of the bloodiest wars in modern history—the four-year American Civil War—and in a ten-year period of post-war turmoil known as Reconstruction. Warned of the consequences of secession by Governor Houston, the delegates and their leaders nevertheless took the Lone Star State out of the Union in a convincing and unhesitating manner.

The town of Austin had taken on a festive air for February 1, and the mood of the day was much in evidence in the noisy crowd that jammed the galleries of "Secession Hall." The floor of the hall, too, was crowded; for not only were all of the convention delegates present, but also the justices of the State Supreme Court and of the District and Federal Courts, and members of both houses of the State Legislature, who had been invited to witness the voting on the Ordinance of Secession. Both the Governor and Lieutenant Governor Edward Clark were invited to attend the proceedings. President Roberts thought that it was particularly important that Houston attend the voting session, that perhaps the magnitude of the vote for secession might impress him. Perhaps the overwhelming vote and the enthusiasm of the delegates and the spectators for secession might even persuade the rugged old lion to favor withdrawal from the Union. With Houston on the side of secession, little formal opposition to the movement in Texas would exist. On the other hand, the chair paid scant attention to Lieutenant Governor Clark, who was already safely in the camp of the secessionists.

As the Governor entered the hall, he was greeted by a ripple of polite applause from the delegates, jurists, and legislators and by a rather noisy greeting of mixed boos and cheers from the less reserved crowd in the galleries. Every possible courtesy was extended by the convention to the Chief Executive. He was escorted into the hall by J. L. Hogg and W. P. Rogers, two of his personal friends (the latter being his cousin); and he was seated to the right of President Roberts—the place of honor. Houston, once seated, folded his arms across his chest and gazed impassively, almost mesmerically, into the sea of faces that faced him. He was to change his physical position and facial expression but little during the entire proceeding.

The special guest seated; Roberts rapped for order; the buzzing subsided; and Secretary Brownrigg read the Ordinance of Secession for the third and last time. The way was now cleared for the vote on secession. Voting in alphabetical order, L. A. Abercrombie, a young lawyer from Walker County, voted first—he voted "yea." Each affirmative vote was greeted with loud cheers, hurrahs, and foot stampings from the spectators in the galleries! Except for an occasional show of emotion, the floor of the hall remained comparatively quiet during the proceedings. Seventy "yeas" were cast before a "nay" was recorded. The first "nay" vote brought an expected outburst of boos and catcalls from the onlookers, which was duly repeated the few times that a negative vote was cast.

T. P. Hughes, a lawyer from Williamson County, cast the first dissenting vote. Only seven other delegates joined Hughes in opposing the Ordinance—J. F. Johnson of Titus County; W. H. Johnson, L. H. Williams, and G. W. Wright of Lamar County; J. D. Rains and A. P. Shuford of Wood County, and J. W. Throckmorton of Collin County. The final count was 166 votes for the Ordinance of Secession and but eight against it. If Sam Houston was perturbed by the overwhelming vote to leave the Union, he did not show it.

Except for the spontaneous reaction of the galleries to the individual votes as they were announced, the voting session, relatively speaking, passed off quietly and smoothly. However, two wholly unexpected and dramatic incidents took place on the floor that involved two of the most respected delegates—both outstanding Texans—T. J. Chambers and J. W. Throckmorton. Thomas Jefferson Chambers, a Virginian who had emigrated to Texas in 1829, and in 1861 was a planter in the county named for him, was the first to break the no-discussion rule laid down by the convention for the voting session. Chambers, incidentally, was the chairman of the Committee on Federal Relations which wrote the Ordinance of Secession. After casting a loud and triumphant "yea" when his name was called, Chambers, a bitter anti-Houstonite, left his seat and advanced threateningly down the aisle toward the Governor. Pointing his finger at the General, he accused him, among other things, of being a traitor. At this juncture of the episode, fellow delegate William P. Rogers, Houston's cousin, sprang to his feet, intercepted Chambers, and forced an apology from the overwrought Virginian. Houston remained unmoved during the verbal explosion and counter-action by Rogers. It is interesting to note that Chambers was murdered at his home in Texas during the latter part of the war, while Rogers was killed gallantly leading the 2nd Texas Infantry at Corinth in late 1862.

The other dramatic and exciting incident that happened during the vote on the Ordinance of Secession is much better known and appears in every Texas history book. It concerned James Webb Throckmorton, a Tennesseean who had emigrated to Texas in 1841, and in 1861 was one of the outstanding lawyers of Collin County. When Throckmorton, the leader of the small pro-Houston minority in the Senate, was called upon to cast his vote, like Chambers before him he broke the no-discussion rule. He rose from his seat and, looking straight at Roberts, said, "Mr. President, in view of the responsibility, in the presence of God and my country—and unawed by the wild spirit of revolution around me, I vote 'nay'." As Throckmorton sat down, he was tendered the customary derisive remarks and hoots reserved for the delegates voting "no," except that the negative reaction to Throckmorton's vote was more prolonged,—he had had the effrontery to defend his vote. Incensed by the reaction, the Collin County lawyer rose to his feet a second time and faced the chair saying, "Mr. President, when the rabble hiss, well may patriots tremble." This stirring, electrifying, Patrick Henry-like remark caused the galleries (although mainly hostile) to break out in prolonged cheering. Throckmorton, however, once Texas had seceded, served the Confederacy and Texas in several important civilian and military capacities.

To make everything extra-legal, the Legislature passed an act on February 7, 1861, legalizing the Ordinance of Secession. With the passing of the Ordinance by the convention and its certification by the Legislature, the secession movement in Texas for all practical purposes was completed. There was never much doubt that the electorate would ratify the decision of their elected representatives.

The day following the passage of the Ordinance of Secession the delegates were presented with an address enumerating the causes that prompted Texas to withdraw from the Union. The address, known officially as the "Declaration of Causes," listed ten major reasons or grievances for the withdrawal that ranged from the Federal government's failure to protect the borders of Texas from the Indians and the Mexicans to the fact that Texas had not been permitted to enjoy the blessings guaranteed to it when it became a member of the Union. All of the delegates who had voted for the Ordinance of Secession the previous day affixed their signatures to the "declaration." In order to give the address the widest possible dissemination, 10,000 copies were published in English, 2,000 in German, and the same number in Spanish.

The only other important order of business transacted by the Convention during its first session was to elect seven men to represent Texas at the convention of the Southern states meeting at Montgomery, Alabama. This illegal step had been taken without waiting for the results of the popular referendum as the delegates had pledged to do. It was at the Montgomery convention that the Southern Confederacy was organized (a provisional Constitution was issued February 8) and Jefferson Davis was elected president (February 9). The seven Texas delegates to Montgomery were John H. Reagan, Louis T. Wigfall, John Hemphill, John Gregg, T. N. Waul, W. S. Oldham, and William B. Ochiltree. Upon their arrival at Montgomery the Texas representatives were seated as members of the Provisional Congress of the Confederate States of America.

The first session of the Texas Convention adjourned February 4, to convene again on March 2. The principle order of business for the second session of the Convention would be to verify the vote of the people cast on February 23. March 2 was selected as the official date for the Ordinance of Secession to take effect as it was the twenty-fifth birthday of Texas—ironically it was also Sam Houston's sixty-eighth birthday. The Convention projected itself between sessions by appointing a select group of nineteen delegates, called the Committee of Public Safety. John C. Robertson of Smith County was president of this powerful committee that was clothed with almost unlimited power by the Convention.

President Roberts, just prior to adjournment on February 5, congratulated the Convention on its courteous and conciliatory deliberations and bade the members go home and appeal to the people "to sustain our action by their votes; and when we reassemble on the 2nd of March let us bring back with us the voice of a united people, in favor of an immediate action to sustain the rights of the people of Texas and of the South at all hazards, and to the last extremity."

The relatively short period of time between sessions of the Convention (February 5-March 1, 1861) was marked by political palaver and military maneuvering. Both the Unionists and the Secessionists had their key speakers canvassing the state for votes. The Unionists, led by the Governor, marshalled their forces for a last-ditch stand. Twenty-five pro-Union members of the Convention and the Legislature banded together and issued an address requesting that the people of Texas oppose secession. Houston, as he had done prior to the meeting of the Convention, made a swing through the strongly secessionist sections of the state for the Unionist cause. Speaking at Waco, the General prophesied that if they voted to go out of the Union grass would soon be growing in their streets. At Gilmer, when asked to give his frank opinion of Thomas Jefferson Green, who was then stumping the state for secession, Houston replied that T. J. Green had "all the characteristics of a dog except fidelity." Defamation of character, slander and personal insults were the order of the day for both factions.

The newspapers were particularly outspoken. As had been the case since states' rights versus federalism first became a public issue in the state during the Houston-Runnels gubernatorial race in mid-1859, most of the big circulation editors were on the side of secession. The most powerful dailies in Texas, Cushing's Houston *Telegraph*, Richardson's Galveston *News*, and Marshall's *State-Gazette* (Austin) were in the corner of the pro-Southern element and were instrumental in moulding the mood of the electorate. Even the conservative Dallas *Herald*, edited by John Swindell, finally joined the anti-Houston forces. The Unionists could count on such papers as *The Southern Intelligencer*, the Bastrop *Adver-*

tiser, the Grange *True Issue* and the *Weekly Alamo Express,* but these journals (except perhaps for *The Southern Intelligencer*) lacked the appeal, the circulation, and the influence of the secession sheets.

A review of the newspapers of the time reveals numerous reports of arbitrary arrests, murders, and the stoning of Unionist speakers during the prelude to the election. A Waco vigilante committee announced that it would hang every Lincoln sympathizer (Unionist) who "bragged" about it. In many communities conservatives or pro-Union advocates were not permitted to congregate or gather in groups of more than a half dozen. There is not much doubt that under community pressure many Union men changed sides—at least at the ballot box.

While the stump speakers harangued for votes the Committee of Public Safety and the Knights of the Golden Circle were busy neutralizing the Federal military posts in the state. In February, 1861, the Federal government maintained nineteen active military posts or stations in the Lone Star State. In fact about 15 per cent (some 2,000 officers and enlisted men) of the National Army was stationed along the western frontier of Texas and the Rio Grande River. Texas comprised the 5th United States Military District with headquarters at San Antonio. The 5th Military District was commanded by Brevet Major General Daniel Emmanuel Twiggs, a veteran of the Second Seminole and the Mexican wars. Twiggs, a Georgian and a secessionist, held the key to Federal military resistance. In December, 1860, Twiggs suddenly returned from sick leave in Louisiana to resume command of the military district that had been temporarily held by Colonel Robert E. Lee. Lee, whose writings and public utterances up to this time had pegged him as a Unionist, was sent to Fort Mason (as commander of the elite 2nd U. S. Cavalry), an isolated post between the Llano and San Saba Rivers, some 150 miles northwest of San Antonio. With Lee out of the way and Twiggs in command, the Texas secessionists expected little resistance to their takeover of the Federal garrisons. They were not to be disappointed.

The Committee of Public Safety designated Ben McCulloch, who had fought under Sam Houston at San Jacinto, as the interim commander of Texas troops. He was ordered to seize the Federal headquarters at San Antonio. Early on the morning of February 16, McCulloch and about 1,000 "buffalo hunters" appeared on the outskirts of San Antonio, surrounded the Federal headquarters, and demanded the surrender of the headquarters personnel, the buildings, and the arsenal. General Twiggs, after balking for a while over terms, agreed to surrender to Texas secessionist authorities not only the San Antonio post but all of the other Federal military stations in the state. Henry E. McCulloch, a brother of

Ben, was assigned the task of taking over the Federal forts in North Texas, and John S. Ford was assigned by the Committee of Public Safety to take the surrender of the posts in South Texas. Thus, without firing a shot (in anger) and by bold action, Texas had put out of action 2,000 Federal troops, had acquired military supplies and other property valued at somewhere between 1.5 and 3 million dollars, and had seized $80,000 in cash. Twiggs had perpetrated the biggest giveaway in American military history. The generous Georgian was relieved of command and was replaced by Colonel C. A. Waite on February 18. Twiggs was cashiered from the United States Army on March 1, 1861, and was promptly rewarded with a major general's commission by the Confederate government.

With the surrender of the Federal garrisons, the last hope of the Texas Unionists for military support in their fight against secession vanished. This stroke of military fortune was hailed with jubilation in the camp of the secessionists, who trooped to the polls in overwhelming numbers on February 23—referendum day. For the demoralized Unionists the surrender of the Federal troops appeared to be the end of their uphill fight to keep Texas in the Federal system. Only a miracle at the ballot box could prevent the ratification of the Ordinance. The miracle failed to materialize.

It was a disorderly referendum. The election machinery in most cases was supervised by the pro-Southern element, and numerous charges were made by Unionists in reference to improper ballot counting and the refusal to permit voting by Union sympathizers. Twenty-seven counties, including some of those having the greatest population, made no official returns until several days after the balloting was over. Of the estimated 80,000 eligible voters in Texas, a little over 60,000 (or 75 per cent) went to the polls. Coercion probably kept some voters away. The final tabulation, as verified on March 4, 1861, during the second session of the Convention, listed 46,129 voting for the Ordinance of Secession and 14,697 against. Thus secession carried by a vote of a little over three to one.

Of the 154 counties in the state at the time, thirty were unorganized. Of the 124 counties eligible to vote, 122 voted; only McCulloch and Presidio counties submitted no returns. Only eighteen counties (concentrated in two areas of the state) voted against the Ordinance. James Throckmorton and his Union associates carried eight counties in northern Texas between the Dallas and Fort Worth area and the Red River. There were few slaves in this area, and many of the settlers had immigrated here from Northern states. The other concentrated number of pro-Union votes came from the Austin area and the counties just west of Austin. Seven counties in this section of the state voted against the Ordinance. Several reasons account for the anti-secession vote in this bloc of counties—the small number of slaves, the large number of German immigrants, and the popularity of Sam Houston in the area. With few exceptions, the heavy slave-holding counties gave large majorities to secession. In seven counties not one vote was recorded against the Ordinance.

At the close of business on February 4, President Roberts had pronounced the Convention adjourned until the following March 2. As programmed, the second session of the Convention did meet in the hall of the House of Representatives on March 2, but lacking a quorum and the following day being Sunday, it adjourned until March 4. As previously stated, it was on this day (March 4) that the vote on the Ordinance was verified and Texas was proclaimed "officially" out of the Union. As the delegates passed out through the south gate of the capitol grounds on their lunch adjournment, they saw posted a proclamation by Governor Houston recognizing the act of secession.

To secede or not to secede from the Union was technically the only question on which the people voted on February 23. However, the Convention interpreted the large vote for secession as a mandate from the people to take the next obvious step—affiliation with the Confederate government recently formed in Montgomery, Alabama. With this step the Governor took violent issue. He had reluctantly gone along with severance from the Union—the voters had approved it and he had officially proclaimed it. The old General, still harboring the idea of the return of Texas to republic status, adamantly refused to recognize all further actions taken by the Convention.

The Convention moved swiftly to tie Texas to the Montgomery government. On March 5, the delegates "approved, ratified, and accepted" the provisional government of the Confederate States of America and instructed their seven-man delegation at Montgomery to seek admission to that government. However, this action was unnecessary, for the Confederate Provisional Congress had passed an act to admit Texas as the eighth state in the Confederacy on March 1. Thus did Texas formally sever her ties with the Federal Union and join the Southern Confederation.

On the following day, March 6, Houston, grasping at every straw in an attempt to sidetrack the inevitable, decried the "illegal" action of the Convention. He reminded the Convention that it had been authorized only to submit the secession question to the people, and nothing more. It was understood, said Houston, "that the performance of the act [canvassing the vote of the people] would terminate the existence of the Convention." The Governor further proclaimed that he would instruct the Legislature when it reconvened on March 18 to make changes in the State Constitution, not for the purpose of joining the Confederacy, but to resume again its independent status. To nullify the Governor's objection, the Convention proceeded to clothe itself with the necessary authority to join the Confederacy or take any other action it deemed necessary under the circumstances. On March 8, the delegates voted unanimously that the Convention had the power to exercise the right "on behalf of the people of Texas to do whatever . . . may be necessary and proper for the protection of the rights of the people and the defense of the State in the present emergency." Taking advantage of its new authority, the Convention proceeded to change the State Constitution to comply with Confederate requirements.

The Convention, angered by the Governor's refusal to submit to its control and fearful that Houston's persuasiveness might induce the Legislature to negate the Convention's actions when it reconvened on March 18, played its trump card. On March 14, the Convention adopted an ordinance to provide for the continuance of the existing state government by requiring all state offiicals to take an oath to the Confederate government. It was implied in the ordinance that refusal to take the oath was tantamount to replacement. Those state officials not present at the Convention were to be notified of the requirement by designated delegates. George W. Chilton, a young Smith County lawyer, was appointed by the chair to deliver to Governor Houston the message that he appear at twelve o'clock noon on March 16 to swear allegiance to the Confederate government.

On Friday evening, March 15, 1861, George Chilton, not finding the Governor at his office in the Capitol, went to the executive mansion to deliver the Convention's ultimatum. The General received Chilton courteously, heard the message, remarked about the short time allowed to think the matter over, and then dismissed the Convention courier without giving an indication as to his intentions.

Nancy Houston, the Governor's eldest daughter, takes the story up from here. After receiving the message from Chilton, the General sat down to dinner and presided over the evening meal. Following supper, as was the custom in the Houston household, the General read a number of passages from the Bible to the family and to the servants who always gathered in the dining room. He then kissed the younger children goodnight and sent them to bed. Later the General went up to his room, telling his wife, Margaret, that he wanted "to think things out." Removing his coat, vest, and finally his shoes so as not to disturb the rest of the household as he paced the floor, the old soldier walked the room while pondering his decision as Margaret waited below. (Houston's actions are reminiscent of those of Robert E. Lee as he paced the bedroom floor of Lee Mansion at Arlington in April, 1861, debating whether or not to resign his commission in the United States Army, while his wife waited below.) Finally the General came downstairs, went in to see his wife, and exclaimed, "Margaret, I will never do it." After making what must have been one of the hardest decisions of his life, Sam Houston retired to his room for the night to commence work on one of his finest state papers—an "Address to the People."

Just before noon on the sixteenth (the day of the required oath), the Governor went to the Capitol and carried with him a soft pine stick and his best whittling knife. Avoiding the crowd that had gathered in the lobby outside of the House Chamber and in front of his office, Houston took a back stairway to the basement. Here he dropped into a chair, took out his knife, and commenced to whittle. Overhead in the hall of the House of Representatives at twelve o'clock sharp Oran Roberts announced that "the hour had arrived for administering the oath of office as prescribed by the ordinance. . . ." Governor Houston's name was the first to be called by Secretary Brownrigg. Four times Brownrigg, in a clear stentorian voice, called out "Sam Houston," and four times he failed to get an answer. With each pronouncement of his name, the Governor cut a long chip off of the pine. Roberts waited a "reasonable time" for the Governor to come forward; and when he did not appear, the names of the other state officers were called. All came forward to take the Confederate oath except E. W. Cave, the Secretary of State. The positions of governor and secretary of state were then declared vacant. That afternoon Edward Clark was sworn in as the new governor of Texas, and Sam Houston went to the executive office in the capitol to commence work on his "Address to the Legislature," ignoring completely Clark's ascension to power.

General Sam Houston's public career, one of the most distinguished careers in American history, came to an end for all practical purposes at high noon on March 16, 1861. However, he wrote two state papers of consequence just before and right after being deposed as governor of Texas. On March 16, Houston issued a broadside entitled "Address to the People." The General had probably started this paper on the night of March 15, after being informed of the required oath to the Confederacy, and finished it on the morning of the sixteenth. This was the last state paper that Sam Houston wrote while governor. Composed as it was on the eve of his deposal, it is a document punctuated with much nostalgia, some bitterness, and a touch of martyrdom. The concluding sentences of the "address" are most poignant and show how deeply Houston was affected by what he considered to be a betrayal of himself and of the Union by the people of Texas. Here are the concluding sentences of Houston's moving Address to the People (of Texas).

> It is perhaps but meet that my career should close thus. I have seen the patriots and statesmen of my youth, one by one, gathered to their fathers, and the Government which they had created, rent in twain; and none like them are left to unite it once again. I stand the last almost of a race, who learned from their lips the lessons of human freedom. I am stricken down now, because I will not yield those principles, which I have fought for and struggled to maintain. The severest pang is that the blow comes in the name of the State of Texas.

The second state paper written immediately after Houston had been replaced as governor was composed sometime between March 16 and March 18, as it was delivered on the latter date to the State Legislature. After five weeks' adjournment, the state lawmakers reconvened on March 18. The lengthy paper that the General delivered on this occasion is generally known as the "Address to the Legislature" and is Houston's last message to a Texas legislative body. The Address to the Legislature is largely a review of Houston's historic, negative position toward the Convention and particularly the Committee of Public Safety. The General referred to the latter as being "high-handed" and the "usurper of the people's rights." He detailed his reasons for not supporting the Confederate government—primarily because the people hadn't voted to join the Southern Association and for this he had been turned out of his legitimate office. The General called upon the now almost powerless and hostile (to him) Legislature to overrule the Convention and to negate its orders as they, the legislators, were the only true representatives of the people. In concluding his address, Houston reminded the legislators that he had the power as commander-in-chief of the state troops to call out the militia, but that would mean civil war in Texas. This step he said he refused to take, but he maintained that he was still the constitutional governor of Texas and would consider himself thus.

Constitutional governor or not, Houston was asked to vacate the governor's mansion on March 18—on the twentieth the General, Margaret, and their eight children moved to a temporary home in Austin before moving to Huntsville.

Although technically deposed as governor on the sixteenth, the General still continued to go each day to the executive office of the Capitol. However, on the morning of March 21, the General was a little late in arriving at his office, and he found Edward Clark occupying the governor's chair. According to a local newspaper story at the time, the conversation between the two "governors" went as follows:

> "Well, *Governor* Clark," said Houston, giving great emphasis to the title, "you are an early riser."
> "Yes, *General*," said Clark, placing great emphasis upon the military title of his predecessor, "I am illustrating the old maxim, the early bird catches the worm."
> "Well, Governor Clark, I hope you will find it an easier seat than I have found it."
> "I'll endeavor to make it so, General, by conforming to the clearly expressed wish of the people of Texas," said Clark.

The newspaper article continued by saying that the General, who had brought a large lunch basket with him, then proceeded to store away in the basket a few personal articles in preparation to vacating the office. Soon he was ready to leave. "Halting at the door, the General made a profound bow and with an air of elaborate dignity said, 'Good-day Governor C-L-A-R-K.' 'Good-day General Houston,' was the Governor's response." Thus was the grizzled old war horse eased from the public scene into political retirement.

Unlike Francis P. Blair, Jr., the Missouri statesman, Sam Houston did not encourage Federal military intervention in Texas' internal affairs, although the opportunity to do so occurred on several occasions. Blair, leader of the Unionist element in Missouri, teamed up with Federal General Nathaniel Lyon to drive the secessionist forces from the state in a series of military engagements. Houston was presented with several opportunities to contest, by armed force, the domination of the Southern element in Texas both during and after his governorship, but he refused to turn Texas into a battleground. On at least two occasions during early and mid-March, 1861, President Lincoln offered to send Federal troops into Texas and place them under Houston's command. Houston was sorely tempted to take Lincoln's second offer (made through George H. Giddings, a Texan); but after consulting with four of the Unionist leaders in the state he decided against it, saying, "Gentlemen, I have asked your advice and will take it, but if I were twenty years younger I would accept Mr. Lincoln's proposition and endeavor to keep Texas in the Union."

In late March, the General declined a third offer of Federal assistance, this one made by the Commander in Chief of the United States Army, Winfield Scott. Scott ordered Colonel Charles A. Waite, (who had replaced Twiggs), to concentrate the some 2,000 Federal troops who were in the process of leaving Texas, at Indianola, providing Houston could and would raise a substantial force of Texas Unionists. The General declined Scott's offer (made through Waite) on March 29, suggesting in his reply that all Federal troops be removed as soon as possible to prevent open conflict in the state. This was Houston's last opportunity to secure Federal military aid to resist the secessionist takeover of Texas.

Two other interesting opportunities for resistance to the pro-Southern forces, besides the three offers for Federal intervention, presented themselves to the General. As governor of the state, Houston was also commander in chief of the state militia. By declaring that a state of emergency existed, the Governor could have called the militia to duty. With the secessionist element as strong as it was, however, it is doubtful if many men would have heeded the call. Such a call could have precipitated civil war in the state. Thus Houston (as he had stated in his Address to the Legislature) declined to exercise his state command authority, fearing such a result.

On the night of March 19, when Houston was packing to leave the executive mansion, a group of armed Unionists gathered outside of the mansion bent on reinstating him in office. The General thanked them for their loyalty, but refused, he said, to make a move that might bring on an armed conflict "merely to keep one poor old man in a position for a few days longer." Houston's love for the Federal Union was great, but his love for Texas was greater—he refused to initiate armed action against his fellow Texans even if it meant saving the state for the Union.

After seceding, Texas went on to play a prominent role in the unsuccessful but gallant Confederate bid for nationhood. Some 60,000 Texans served with regular Confederate Army units. Texas Confederate organizations, the most famous of which were probably Hood's Texas Brigade (1st, 4th and 5th Texas Infantry Regiments) and Terry's Texas Rangers (8th Texas Cavalry Regiment), gained fame in all three theaters of operation. Another estimated 10,000 to 15,000 Texans served in state defense units that guarded the Indian frontier, the Rio Grande River, the 600-mile Gulf Coast, and the Northeast Texas Federal invasion routes. No other Southern state faced the serious internal security problem that Texas did. The Lone Star State furnished thirty-one *bona fide* generals to the Confederate Army, including two full generals—Albert Sidney Johnston and John Bell Hood, the latter, a Texan by declaration. John H. Reagan served as Postmaster General for Jefferson Davis, while ex-Governor Francis Lubbock served the Confederate President as advisor on Trans-Mississippi affairs. Texas furnished much beef and grain to the Southern Army, and Texas cotton helped to pay for badly needed war materials from abroad. Although no major battle was fought on Texas soil, Dick Dowling's defense of Sabine Pass (September 8, 1863) must rank as one of the great military feats of the war. While the first land engagement of the bloody four-year conflict was fought in the East (Philippi, Virginia, on June 3, 1861), fittingly enough the last land engagement was fought in the West—Palmito Ranch, Texas, on May 13, 1865.

Jefferson Davis, on welcoming Texas troops to Virginia in October, 1861, had stated, "Texans! The troops of other states have their reputtions to gain; the sons of the defenders of the Alamo have theirs to maintain! I am assured that you will be faithful to the trust." Although fighting in a losing cause, the high military reputations of the Texans *was maintained*—they were faithful to the trust!